Migration and social mobility

The life chances of Britain's minority ethnic communities

Migration and social mobility

The life chances of Britain's minority ethnic communities

Lucinda Platt

JOSEPH ROWNTREE
FOUNDATION

First published in Great Britain in November 2005 by

The Policy Press
Fourth Floor, Beacon House
Queen's Road
Bristol BS8 1QU
UK

Tel no +44 (0)117 331 4054
Fax no +44 (0)117 331 4093
Email tpp-info@bristol.ac.uk
www.policypress.org.uk

Published for the Joseph Rowntree Foundation by The Policy Press

ISBN 1 86134 800 2

British Library Cataloguing in Publication Data
A catalogue record for this book is available from the British Library.

Library of Congress Cataloging-in-Publication Data
A catalog record for this book has been requested.

Lucinda Platt is Lecturer in Sociology at the University of Essex.

The **Joseph Rowntree Foundation** has supported this project as part of its programme of research and innovative development projects, which it hopes will be of value to policy makers, practitioners and service users. The facts presented and views expressed in this report are, however, those of the author and not necessarily those of the Foundation.

The statements and opinions contained within this publication are solely those of the author and not of The University of Bristol or The Policy Press. The University of Bristol and The Policy Press disclaim responsibility for any injury to persons or property resulting from any material published in this publication.

The Policy Press works to counter discrimination on grounds of gender, race, disability, age and sexuality.

Cover design by Qube Design Associates, Bristol
Printed in Great Britain by Hobbs the Printers Ltd, Southampton

Contents

List of tables and figures

Tables

Figures

Acknowledgements

I am grateful to the Office for National Statistics (ONS) for accepting my proposal to Beta Test the ONS Longitudinal Study (ONS LS) 2001 Census data, on which this research is based. I am also grateful to CeLSIUS and Julian Buxton in particular, for facilitating my access to the ONS LS, for responding to queries and for checking innumerable lengthy output files. I would also like to thank Alec Ross, of ONS, who encouraged me to undertake the Beta Test and supported my application, and who has since cleared various outputs resulting from the research.

The Joseph Rowntree Foundation generously supported this research under their Census programme. I am grateful to them and to Anne Harrop in particular for the interest she showed in the project. I would also like to thank all the members of the advisory group who gave of their time to make invaluable comments and suggestions: Bola Akinwale, David Blackaby, Anthony Heath, James Nazroo and Mike Savage.

Preliminary results from this research were presented at the launch of the ONS LS in September 2004. I am grateful to all participants at that event for their comments and questions. I would also like to thank participants of a seminar at the University of Bath and colleagues at the University of Essex, in particular Stephen Jenkins, for their comments.

The Policy Press have, once again, been a pleasure to work with and I would like to thank all those involved in seeing this report through to publication.

Introduction

Background

While Britain has always been a country of immigration and some of its minority group populations have been here for an extremely long period, the current minority ethnic populations are largely the result of immigration in the post-war period from former colonies or Commonwealth countries (Solomos, 1989; Goulborne, 1998; Mason, 2000). The experience of these immigrant populations and their children and grandchildren has been a mixed one, and the different groups show great diversity in terms of income, employment, educational achievement and life chances (Modood et al, 1997; Platt, 2002; Mason, 2003).

This diversity will be in part a consequence of factors associated with the processes of migration: the reason for migration; the different economic, social and human capital that the migrants brought with them; the stage of life and the point in time at which migration occurred and the opportunities available at that time. But it is also likely that the diversity has been shaped by the experience of the different groups over time in Britain: the length of time spent in Britain; the characteristics of the areas of settlement – and the possibilities for geographical mobility within Britain; the experience of racism, and responses to it; interaction with the education system and the labour market over time. When exploring the experience of the 'second' (non-migrant) generation, this leads to a consideration of whether different groups' social and economic origins – the situation of their parents and what their parents brought with them in terms of economic resources and human capital (education/qualifications) – are crucial in explaining their outcomes and the diversity between groups. Or, conversely, are parental origins less important than distinct intersections of location, discrimination and even onward migration experienced by the different populations within Britain?

There have been a number of explanations put forward to account both for differences between generations of the same ethnic group in a particular country and for the long-term outcomes of different ethnic groups. It is argued that the migrant generation can be expected to differ from the succeeding generation, born and brought up in the country of immigration, in a number of (possibly conflicting) ways, within which the migrant's migration history and own characteristics are given different degrees of attention. Initially, lack of networks and familiarity with the 'host' community can be expected to depress the occupational achievement of the migrants, relative to their skills and education. This may be exacerbated if the migration was forced rather than voluntary. In this model, assimilation will lead to the second generation being much closer to their peers from the host community in educational and occupational terms (Park, 1950; see also Gordon, 1964; and Alba and Nee, 1997).

While at the institutional and analytical level assimilation has been less fully endorsed in British accounts, we have seen a related argument for the 'recovery' of the underlying or latent class position of the first generation in the second generation (for example, Modood, 1997a; see also Heath and McMahon (2005) for a consideration of the international salience of higher-class origins). Groups, such as Indians or Chinese, who (or some of who) had more highly skilled and highly educated origins and were more likely to experience downward migration on arrival, were seen as reasserting their backgrounds in the second generation; while those whose class position on arrival in Britain showed greater continuity with a less skilled background were seen as continuing to remain at the less skilled end of the class spectrum in future generations. This argument has been used in particular to explain the high levels of achievement of Indians and African Asians in successive generations. Indeed, the separation between African Asians and Indians in the *Fourth*

National Survey of Ethnic Minorities was informed by, as well as reinforcing, such a perspective (Modood et al, 1997).

Daniel (1968) drew attention to the extent of downward mobility experienced by immigrants following their entry into Britain. The lack of transparent congruence between qualifications and occupational class (Heath and Ridge, 1983; Modood, 1997b) is also taken as some evidence of downward mobility in the migrant generation. Alternatively, Smith (1977) emphasised how migrants employed in particular occupational niches, such as Pakistanis employed in the textile industry, may be accounted for by prior experience. The role of geographical factors – the influence of area or region of initial settlement of migrants – has also been considered important in shaping or mediating outcomes for the second generation (Galster et al, 1999; see also Dorsett, 1998). Such areas of settlement are themselves not independent of the period of migration, opportunities for employment in different areas, and the match between those opportunities and the skills that the migrants bring with them. In so far as location of initial settlement and subsequent geographical mobility varies by migrant group, it is likely to result in systematic differences in the experiences of different minority ethnic groups in the longer term. Such evidence has contributed to an argument that the current occupational profiles of minority ethnic groups may owe much to their pre-migration history.

Moreover, migrants are acknowledged as a selected sample, who may have particular levels of motivation that caused them to migrate in the first place, but that may not be directly passed on to their children. This could mean that the second generation might be expected to fare less well than their parents in occupational terms, particularly if the children find that being born and bred in a country does not exempt them from racism and discrimination. The poor health status of certain minority groups in Britain, has, on occasion been discussed in these terms (see, for example, Marmot et al, 1984; Nazroo, 1997).

A perspective that amalgamates aspects of both the assimilation thesis and the relevance of pre-migration history and background suggests that it is crucial what migrant parents bring with them and what they transmit to their children in terms of aspirations and determination to succeed in the context of and interacting with a specific social and institutional (and often hostile) environment (see, for example, Modood, 2004). Such a perspective, without endorsing a beneficent assimilation process, nevertheless locates potential for relative success within the second generation, but links it to particular, selected characteristics of the parents. Specifically, parental commitment to education and to achieving upward mobility through education is regarded as critical, and certain groups are identified as especially likely to hold – or reveal – such a commitment (Archer and Francis, forthcoming). The problem with this position is that commitment to educational success is easier to express in the context of actual educational success, which may, in fact, be linked to non-ethnic group-specific factors. It could be that a group's sense of educational achievement shapes the construction of internal group identity rather than a pre-existing group-based commitment to educational success driving the educational achievement of successive generations.

While there is some support for all of these arguments in the wider literature; in the British context, the complexity of the issue and practical constraints of measurement and investigation have tended to limit the possibilities for determining their relative strength. Which account holds best for Britain's ethnic minorities, for understanding their relative positions in the course of the transition from "immigrant groups to new ethnic minorities" (Castles, 2000) will tend to shift with the way the first and second generations are defined, and according to which ethnic group is the principal focus of interest.

Exploring patterns of intergenerational mobility, the way that parents' and children's occupational/class outcomes relate to one another is one way of gaining a more developed grasp of such questions; and therefore of understanding trends and policy implications. However, while there is a vast body of research into social mobility in Britain generally (see, for example, Goldthorpe et al, 1987; Marshall et al, 1997; Prandy 1998; Bottero and Prandy, 2000; Heath and Payne, 2000; Savage, 2000), and the way it is mediated by education specifically (for example, Halsey et al, 1980), our understanding of the processes of social mobility as they differ by ethnic group and the causes of such differences is extremely limited.

There are few British sources that can directly relate parents' and children's outcomes for minority ethnic groups. (But see the discussion of Anthony Heath's work, below. Even here, however, cross-sectional data with retrospective reporting rather than truly longitudinal data were used.) Therefore, for the purpose of understanding change across time and between groups and developing inferences, 'first' and 'second' generations tend to be constructed from cross-sections of minority groups at successive time points (for example, Modood, 1997a; Robinson, 1990). Obviously in such cases, the 'first generation' are not strictly speaking the parents of the 'second generation', and the probability that the two even approximate to migrant parents and their British-born children will vary with ethnic group (and migration histories). If ethnic groups are still forming and expanding, then the later time point will capture new migrants as well as the 'second generation'. If the group is subject to substantial return or onward migration, many of the potential second generation from the first time point will have been lost. Moreover, the point in their career at which they are measured will contribute to whether upward mobility is observed or not, with those who are younger being less likely to have reached their final class destination.

In addition, the stage at which 'success' is achieved may vary by ethnic group: substantial investment in education may produce later returns. (Such differences in the timing of educational achievement can be observed, for example, in the Youth Cohort Study; see, for example, DfES, 2001.) While it is of inherent interest to observe the changing profile of a group over time by examining succeeding cross-sections, it is more difficult to make confident claims about processes involved in shaping those profiles. I have illustrated these points about the complexity of comparing cross-sections in Figure 1.1 overleaf. The intervening processes in the oval to the right identify those which are of inherent interest in studying social mobility and which are, in theory, measurable through directly relating parents' characteristics and their children's outcomes as adults. Those in the oval to the left are factors that may distort apparent mobility patterns when mobility is inferred through comparison of cross-sections.

Work by Anthony Heath and collaborators has made use of some of the few available sources for the direct measurement of social mobility between parents and children. In engaging directly with parent-to-child mobility by ethnic group using cross-sectional sources with retrospective report of parents' (or, more commonly, father's) occupation, he has illustrated, for example, both differences by

ethnic group and the international salience of 'service' class origins (Heath and Ridge, 1983; Heath and McMahon, 2005). However, in the former case, the relationship that was being measured was that between the migrant's parents' class and the migrant's own occupational situation in Britain. Heath and Ridge (1983) thus showed the levels of downward mobility relative to their parents' background that ethnic minorities faced in Britain. In the latter case, the respondents were a mixture of migrants themselves and second generation, but there was no distinction between whether class of origin was being measured pre- or post-migration (in most cases, it was in fact pre-migration). Thus, Heath and McMahon (2005) illustrated how migrants' backgrounds were important in their occupational attainment, but that an 'ethnic penalty' nevertheless still prevailed. However, they could not take account of potential international non-correspondence of classes nor of what the processes of class mobility had been following migration. In both these important articles, as a result, the contribution of processes operating *within Britain* could not be elucidated.

In summary, most of the ethnically differentiated research has consisted of comparisons of cross-sections, and most of the direct research into intergenerational mobility has been non-ethnically differentiated. And even those rare studies that have measured mobility for different ethnic groups directly are problematic in terms of comparison, as parental class may be measured pre-migration. Such intergenerational mobility studies are therefore not directly comparable with most cross-sections or with non-ethnically differentiated studies. A move in the direction of producing a study that filled this gap was provided by Platt (2005). The research described and reported here pursued that approach, and substantially extended and developed it.

What can this study add?

This Report makes an original contribution to discussions of minority group experience in Britain and transitions between the immigrant and the 'second' generations by observing and analysing actual parent-to-child social-class transitions by ethnic group, where class is measured in Britain for both parents and children. That is, it exploits genuinely longitudinal data to track intergenerational transitions. It makes an innovative contribution to the literature on minority ethnic

Figure 1.1: The factors complicating measurement of mobility through use of comparison of cross-sections

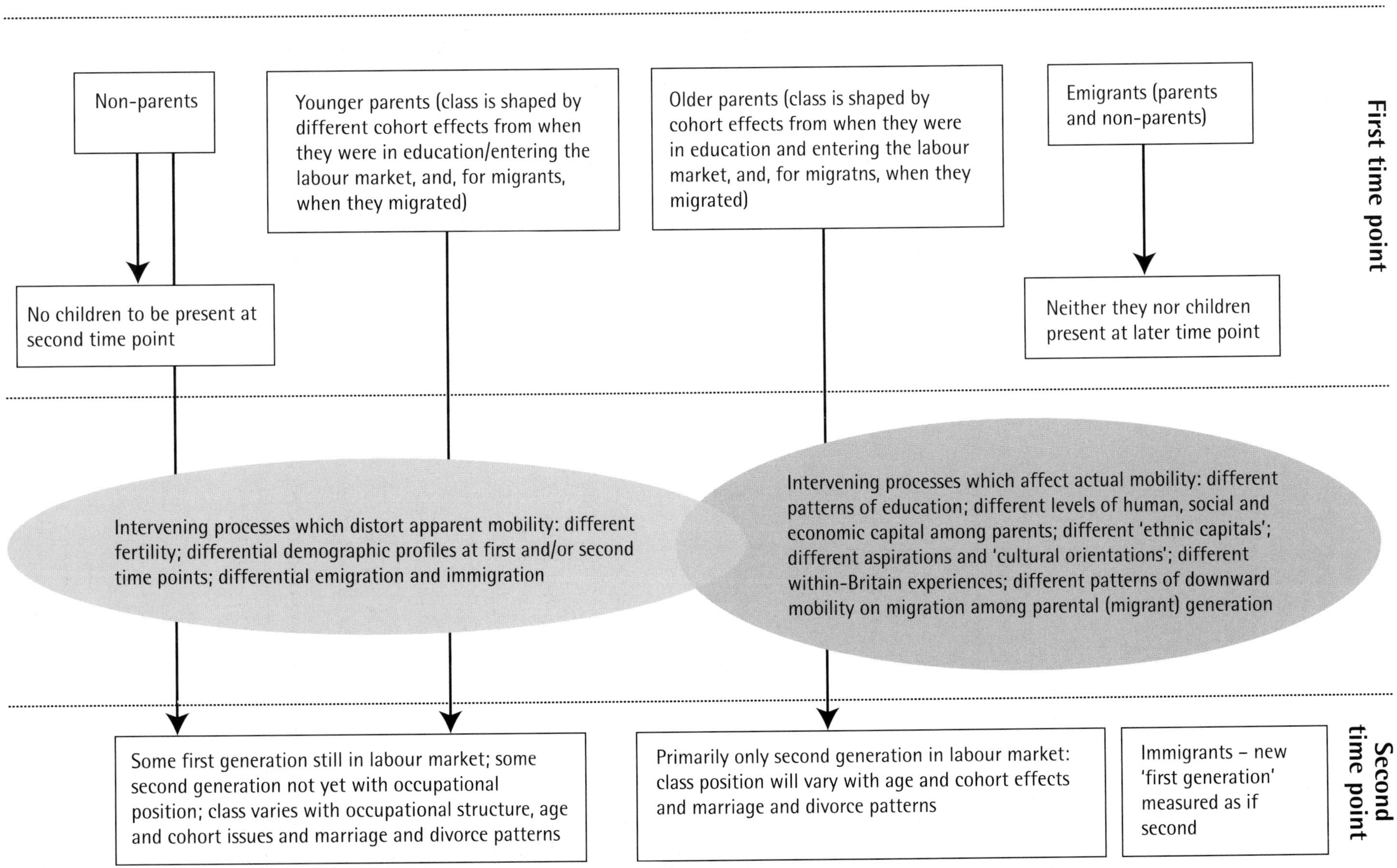

First time point

Second time point

Emigrants (parents and non-parents)

Neither they nor children present at later time point

Immigrants – new 'first generation' measured as if second

Older parents (class is shaped by different cohort effects from when they were in education and entering the labour market, and, for migratns, when they migrated)

Intervening processes which affect actual mobility: different patterns of education; different levels of human, social and economic capital among parents; different 'ethnic capitals'; different aspirations and 'cultural orientations'; different within-Britain experiences; different patterns of downward mobility on migration among parental (migrant) generation

Primarily only second generation in labour market: class position will vary with age and cohort effects and marriage and divorce patterns

Younger parents (class is shaped by different cohort effects from when they were in education/entering the labour market, and, for migrants, when they migrated)

Intervening processes which distort apparent mobility: different fertility; differential demographic profiles at first and/or second time points; differential emigration and immigration

Some first generation still in labour market; some second generation not yet with occupational position; class varies with occupational structure, age and cohort issues and marriage and divorce patterns

Non-parents

No children to be present at second time point

group class distributions and outcomes by demonstrating such direct parent-to-child class transitions across the 'first' and 'second' generations, rather than inferring them from comparisons of cross-sections from different periods.

It observes children growing up in England and Wales of similar ages and thus comparable education and employment histories from different ethnic groups, with destinations measured at the same point in time for all of them. They are therefore suited to comparison of their patterns of origins as they relate to their destinations, without the complicating issues of period and cohort effects, that is, without differential influence from the point in time at which characteristics are measured or from having an earlier rather than a later birth date.[1] It shows the patterns of class mobility for a large sample of children of study members whose class is measured in 2001 and compared with that of their parents measured in 1971 or 1981, when they were at – or about to start – school in England and Wales. It therefore illuminates understanding of the relationship between ethnicity and class origins without necessitating any assumptions about the international comparability of classes.

It asks the fundamental questions:

- Do patterns of intergenerational social mobility vary by ethnic group?
- If so, what are the relative roles of differential class background, migration effects and the 'ethnic penalty' in explaining such differences?
- Are outcomes mediated by educational achievement in the second generation?

Engaging with discussions around the importance of religion in shaping life chances, and taking advantage of the new question on religion in the 2001 Census in England and Wales, it also asks:

- Do patterns of intergenerational mobility vary by religious affiliation?
- What can religion add to our understanding of ethnic group differences?

The Report offers a chance better to understand some of the key issues facing research into ethnic group diversity, disadvantage and success.

Data and methods[2]

To explore these issues, this study uses the ONS Longitudinal Study. The ONS Longitudinal Study (henceforth the LS) is a one per cent sample of the population of England and Wales that is followed over time. It was initially obtained by taking a sample of the 1971 Census, based on those born on one of four birth dates (day and month). Information from samples taken at each subsequent Census has been added to the study. Members are also added to the study between Censuses by linking information on births and immigrations using the same selection criteria. Data on events that occur to sample members – births of children to them, infant deaths, deaths of spouses and cancer registrations – are also added. No more information is linked where study members' records indicate that they have died or left England and Wales (unless emigrants re-enter at a later date, in which case they are re-incorporated into the study).

The ONS Longitudinal Study has some key advantages when it comes to exploring intergenerational mobility and ethnicity, namely the size of the study sample, which facilitates analysis by ethnic group at relatively disaggregated levels, and the longitudinal design of the study, which allows intergenerational mobility to be tracked directly.

For this study, two cohorts of children aged between four and 15 at the point they were observed in the LS have been selected from both the 1971 and the 1981 records in the LS. They are called the '1971 cohort' and the '1981 cohort', based on the point at which they were first observed in the LS for selection into this study. Their parents' and household characteristics are measured at that point to give information about their 'origins'; and their own characteristics are measured in 2001 to given information about their 'destinations'. These two cohorts of children have been combined, or 'pooled', for the majority of the analysis in this Report. Table 1.1 shows the numbers in each of these two cohorts and in the pooled sample for the different minority ethnic groups. The table illustrates how different groups' migration histories mean that the distributions of minority groups are very different for the two cohorts. For example, Indians, Pakistanis and Bangladeshis clearly experienced an increase in

---

[1] For a further discussion of these issues see the Technical Appendix to this Report (available at www.jrf.org.uk/bookshop).

[2] For a more detailed account of the methodological issues see the Technical Appendix (available at www.jrf.org.uk/bookshop).

Table 1.1: Numbers from minority ethnic groups in the samples selected for study from the ONS LS

Ethnic group*	1971 cohort (those aged 4–15 in 1971)	1981 cohort (those aged 4–15 in 1981)	Pooled 1971 and 1981 cohorts
Caribbean	803	744	1,547
Black African	58	94	152
Indian	568	1,123	1,691
Pakistani	173	606	779
Bangladeshi	21	109	130
Chinese and other	197	384	581
White of migrant parentage	2,157	1,518	3,675

Note: *The process used to allocate ethnic group to the sample members and the groups used is discussed further in the Technical Appendix (available at www.jrf.org.uk/bookshop).

Source: ONS LS, author's analysis

migration between 1971 and 1981, while Caribbean immigration declined. The effect of pooling the two cohorts means that the age range when destinations are measured in 2001 will range from 24 to 45. The differences in age are captured in the analysis through adjusting for both age group and cohort. Alternative approaches, for example measuring the cohorts 'after two decades' (that is in 1991 for the 1971 cohort, and in 2001 for the 1981 cohort), or focusing on only the older members of the cohorts (that is those aged between eight and 15 at the point they were first observed) have also been explored, and are discussed in the Technical Appendix (available at www.jrf.org.uk/bookshop). The results and implications of the alternative approaches are also illustrated there.

Parents' social class was measured in 1971 and 1981 respectively for the two cohorts; and, grouped in three categories – service, intermediate and working – was used to identify children's origins. The sample's own social class (their destinations) was measured in 2001 grouped into three corresponding classes (professional/ managerial, intermediate, and manual/routine non-manual) with unemployment forming a fourth outcome. The social class classification used for origins was the CASMIN schema (sometimes known as the Goldthorpe class schema) and that used for destinations was the National Statistics Socio-economic Classification (NS-SeC). Both employ similar principles and approaches in class allocation and are therefore broadly comparable over time. Those parents or children who did not fit one of these social class categories (or unemployment for destinations) were left in a residual, 'other' category, while those for whom there was insufficient information to allocate class at all were

excluded from analysis. Other variables that were included in the analyses were economic status, area and educational level of the study sample's parents, and educational level, marital status, economic status and religion of the study sample. The derivation, creation and harmonisation of these variables is discussed further in the Technical Appendix to the Report (available at www.jrf.org.uk/bookshop).

For analysing the relationship between social class origins and destinations, and the mediating effects of ethnicity, age and education, a variety of methods has been used from simple tabulations and percentages to binomial and multinomial logistic regressions. As far as possible the results of these methods have been presented in illustrative figures or simple tables, with the full results in tabular form included in the Appendix. Additional analyses carried out to test the robustness of the responses to different ways of organising the data have been included in the Technical Appendix (available at www.jrf.org.uk/bookshop).

Note on terminology

The following words or phrases are used in the Report in the following way:

- 'sample members' or 'study members' = those aged 4–15 in 1971 or 1981 who make up the study sample on which this analysis is based, who are followed over time and who constitute a subset of all LS members.
- '1971 cohort' = those aged 4–15 in 1971 and living with at least one parent who were selected for the study. The year 1971 is the time point at which their 'origins' are observed.
- '1981 cohort' = those aged 4–15 in 1981 and living with at least one parent who were selected for the study. The year 1981 is the time point at which their 'origins' are observed.
- 'origins' = parental social class, or other parental characteristics as specified (eg 'housing tenure at origin' = the housing tenure of the household in which the sample member and their parent(s) were living when the sample member was aged 4–15).
- 'destinations' = achieved social class of sample member in 2001; or other sample member's characteristics as specified (eg 'destination housing tenure' = housing tenure of the household in which the sample member was living in 2001).
- 'class transitions' = the sample members' movement from origin class to destination class; similarly
- 'class retention' = sample members remaining in the same social class as that of their parents.

2

Origins and destinations: social mobility and the changing social structure of England and Wales

Previous findings

There is a large body of work that has shown that, within Britain and beyond, there is substantial association between a parent's and child's social class and that this association has persisted even with the expansion of the middle class in the post-war period. The existence of 'more room at the top' has opened up chances for upward mobility from the working classes, but has also made it easier for those from middle-class backgrounds to retain their advantaged class position (Goldthorpe et al, 1987; Erikson and Goldthorpe, 1993; see also the discussion in Aldridge, 2001). The relative odds of ending up in the more privileged social classes thus remain firmly in favour of those with more privileged backgrounds, even though there is some suggestion that this association between privileged background and advantaged outcomes might be gradually weakening (Heath and Payne, 2000). These differential life chances according to social class background are taken to indicate that Britain is a closed society, rather than a 'meritocracy' (Blair, 2001; Aldridge, 2001). However, a society can be closed on other levels than that of class; and levels of intergenerational class stability among minority groups comparable to those of the majority can be read as indicative of greater openness within society to ethnic minority achievement (Hout, 1984). If the impact of origins on chances of professional positions are the same across groups, this suggests that, while we may not be seeing a meritocracy, class does override ethnic differences in outcome, implying lack of ethnic discrimination in occupations. However, if the impact of origins varies between groups and is weaker for some minority groups than for the majority, this will tend

to suggest that class privilege is an insufficient buffer against ethnically based discriminatory processes.

This chapter describes, and explores possible explanations for, mobility patterns among the different ethnic groups considered in this study. It builds on the small body of research examining intergenerational mobility by ethnic group (Heath and Ridge, 1983; Heath and McMahon, 2005; Platt, 2005), but provides a new perspective and findings, which are developed in the analysis which follows in Chapter 3. Heath and Ridge (1983) used the Oxford Mobility Study to compare father–son transitions across English-born non-migrants and four groups of migrants, including a 'non-white' migrant group. They found that there was, for non-white migrants as a whole, a weaker association between origins and destinations than for the British-born and for the white migrant groups. Specifically, higher social class origins abroad did not seem to be carried over into Britain. They concluded that 'non-white' migrants were disadvantaged in the British labour market.

Heath and McMahon (2005) used pooled years from the General Household Survey to assess the contribution of parent's class, ethnicity and educational qualifications to a series of class outcomes. They concluded that patterns of access to different class positions are distinct across ethnic groups and are complex. At the same time the salience of a background in the salariat in terms of access to occupations in the salariat was found to be generalised across ethnic groups. However, these studies focused on mobility regardless of where origin class was measured – in fact it was usually the class in the country of emigration. They therefore both assumed an international comparability of class position and could not tell us about the comparative intergenerational experience of groups *within Britain*, where the specific occupational structure (and the changes that take place within it) will impact on all groups – and might be expected to do so in similar ways. Migrant groups' cultural capital, their expectations and capabilities for particular occupational/class positions prior to migration may be very important in subsequent experience. However, to assume an international salience of class and measure across the point of migration can only give us part of the picture and does not explain if and how groups recover from downward mobility following migration. This Report aims to give the other side of the picture, by exploring how what we know about the migrant generation following their arrival in Britain translates into particular outcomes for the second generation.

Platt (2005) analysed mobility by ethnic group within England and Wales, using an approach that was partly similar to that employed in this Report. However, that paper considered only one cohort, which limited the number of ethnic groups it was possible to investigate, and analysed mobility patterns only up to 1991. Moreover, in its dependence on aggregate data and a restricted range of variables, the paper was not able to extend the analysis into a consideration of factors mediating transmission of origins and destinations, in the ways developed further in the next chapter. The conclusion of this earlier research using the ONS Longitudinal Study (henceforth the LS) was that the relationship between origins and destinations for women remains similar for minority and majority ethnic groups, suggesting that class operates in predictable ways across and within ethnicities for women. However, for men it seemed that intergenerational class patterns were not comparable across ethnic groups, suggesting that for men ethnic group effects override class origins in determining destinations. When the analysis was repeated for the 1981 cohort as part of this study,

Table 2.1: Percentages of each parental class (origins) of the two cohorts (row percentages)

	Service class	Intermediate class	Working class	Other
1971 cohort	24.3	18.3	53.0	4.4
1981 cohort	29.6	18.5	46.2	5.7

Source: ONS LS, author's analysis

the comparable class effects across ethnicity previously observed for women could no longer be found. Instead class effects seemed to vary with ethnic group for both women and men, suggesting that distinctive ethnic group relationships to class origins effects persisted within the younger age group – and for women as well as for men.

The changing occupational structure

This chapter focuses on describing the mobility patterns of the pooled 1971 and 1981 cohorts, measuring their outcomes in 2001. First I examine the occupational structure as it changes over the period of the study. Table 2.1 shows the class origins of the study sample broken down by cohort. We can see from this table how between 1971 and 1981 the class profile of the parents reflects the changes in occupational structure that have been taking place across the period, with the expansion of the service-class at the expense of the working class.

When looking at the destinations, in Table 2.2, we see that the pattern of destinations for the two cohorts is remarkably similar, despite the age differences between them, for the 1971 cohort aged between 34 and 45 in 2001 and the 1981 cohort aged between 24 and 35. Given that the youngest of the 1981 cohort, those aged 24–27, are less likely to have reached their final class position by 2001, the destinations have also been measured excluding this group: the results remain broadly comparable but bring the two cohorts closer

Table 2.2: Proportions of the two cohorts in different destination classes in 2001 (row percentages)

	Professional/managerial	Intermediate	Working	Unemployed	Other
1971 cohort	48.4	19.7	22.9	2.3	6.6
1981 cohort	47.4	18.0	23.7	3.3	7.5
1981 cohort older age groups only	48.6	18.2	23.0	3.0	7.2

Source: ONS LS, author's analysis

Table 2.3: Change in occupational structure between 1971/81 and 2001 (row percentages)

	Service/professional	Intermediate	Working/manual and routine	Unemployed	Other
1971/81	26.3	18.2	49.7	N/A (included in other)	5.8
2001	47.9	18.9	23.3	2.8	7.1

Source: ONS LS, author's analysis

Figure 2.1: The changing class distribution for the study sample compared with their parents, 1971/81 to 2001

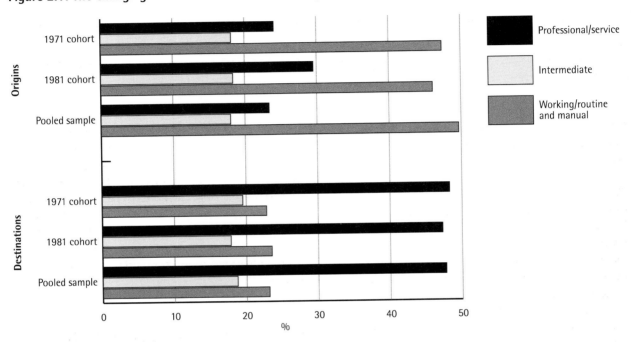

Source: ONS LS, author's analysis

together in their overall patterns of destinations, as might be expected.

Combining the information for both cohorts (the pooled sample) and for both origins and destinations illustrates the overall shifts in class distributions from the parents' to the children's generations. This has been done in Table 2.3, which gives some indication of the changing class structure over the period. What we see here is the expansion of the professional and managerial classes (or the service-class as it was previously called) at the expense of the working (routine and manual) class. These cross-sectional proportions are measured from the parents and children in this study, thus they do not correspond exactly to cross-sectional measures of class or occupational structure at the two time points which would include all those of working age.[3] Nevertheless, the general trends are consistent with the shift towards professionalised occupations over this period.

Table 2.3 shows that, while nearly half of the parents were in working-class occupations, fewer than a quarter of the study members were by 2001. Conversely, by 2001 nearly half of the study members were in professional and managerial occupations. Figure 2.1 summarises the information

---

3   The differences are that the basis of the origin measures are parents only, which will restrict the age range, in addition to the fact that parents do not have an identical distribution to non-parents. For the destinations, the distribution is restricted to those between the ages of 24 and 45. Moreover, for both origins and destinations, the class allocation has been hierarchical where the parents or respondents are part of a couple, rather than individual, that is, the higher class of the pair has been selected, which biases the class distribution upwards compared to an individualised occupational measure (see the Technical Appendix (available at www.jrf.org.uk/bookshop) for further discussion of the construction of the class variables). In addition, 13,863 study members who were aged 4–5 in 1971 are measured twice, since if present in 1981, they were aged 14–15 then.

Table 2.4: Ethnic group distributions, pooled sample, 2001

Ethnic group	Number – all	%	Number for whom both origin and destination class available*	%
White non-migrant	125,014	88.5	106,843	89.1
Caribbean	1,547	1.1	1,069	0.9
Indian	1,691	1.2	1,378	1.2
Pakistani	779	0.6	608	0.5
White migrant	3,675	2.6	2,867	2.4
Other groups** (combined)	8,597	6.0	7,093	6.0
Total	141,303	100	119,858	100

Notes: * Excluding those allocated to the residual 'other' class at either origin or destination.

** These groups are Bangladeshi, Chinese, other ethnic groups, and white where one parent was born abroad and one was born in the UK.

Source: ONS LS, author's analysis

from the previous three tables in graphical form to illustrate the changing class structure between the parents' and children's generations of this study.

These structural changes in the class distribution drive mobility rates for all groups to a greater or lesser extent. That is, they require that a certain proportion of those from working-class backgrounds move up a class or two. Even if all the second generation working class were from working-class backgrounds, around half of those from working-class backgrounds would still have to have changed class by 2001. This has led to the focus in much of the literature on relative mobility chances (for example, Heath and Payne, 2000; although there are some dissenters, such as Payne, 1992, and Payne and Roberts, 2002). Such a focus removes the impact of the purely structural changes, and explores instead the likelihood of achieving a certain class position for someone from a lower class compared to the chances for someone from a higher class. Such research has shown that even if there is, in absolute terms, much upward mobility for those from working-class origins (as the class distribution changes and there are simply fewer working-class jobs), the relative chances of a professional class outcome for those from working-class origins may still be weak compared to those from a service-class background.

Similarly, when examining minority ethnic groups it is worth examining both their absolute and their relative mobility chances. Particularly in view of the effects of downward mobility after immigration, discussed above, a preponderance of working-class origins is likely to lead to much upward mobility. Nevertheless, the amount of absolute mobility may vary between groups with some apparently better

able than others to take advantage of the greater 'room at the top' offered by the changing occupational structure. Upward mobility for minority ethnic groups is likely to be driven, in part at least, by relative concentration among parents in the reducing working class. Alternatively, if upward mobility is not observed, it might lead to the formulation of notions of a residualised working class with an over-representation of minority ethnic groups.

Class transitions from origins to destinations

Table 2.4 shows that the total pooled sample under consideration amounts to 141,303, and also shows the sizes of the ethnic groups that are the main focus in this Report and for which the mobility patterns are illustrated below. However, the number for whom both origin class and destination class information is available is a reduced set of these groups, the numbers being given in a separate column of Table 2.4.

Table 2.5 shows transitions between origins and destinations for the whole study sample. We can see from this table the high levels of class retention for those from service-class backgrounds: 69% of them end up in the professional/managerial classes, whereas under 50% of the intermediate and working class attain a professional/managerial class position.

There are correspondingly small proportions of those from service-class origins who end up in the working class (under 13%). The fairly high levels of

Table 2.5: Social class destinations 2001 according to social class origins 1971/81 (row percentages)

| | | Destinations (2001) | | | | | |
		Professional/ managerial	Intermediate	Routine/ manual	Unemployed	Total (N)	Column %
Origins (1971/1981)	Service	68.9	16.6	12.6	1.8	34,777	29.0
	Intermediate	49.2	24.5	23.8	2.5	23,353	19.5
	Working	43.9	21.0	31.6	3.5	61,728	51.5
	Total	52.2	20.4	24.6	2.8	119,858	100

Source: ONS LS, author's analysis

Table 2.6: Social class destinations 2001 according to social class origins (row percentages): white non-migrants

| | | Destinations (2001) | | | | | |
		Professional/ managerial	Intermediate	Routine/ manual	Unemployed	Total (N)	Column %
Origins (1971/1981)	Service	68.7	16.8	12.8	1.7	31,301	29.3
	Intermediate	48.8	24.5	24.3	2.4	21,070	19.7
	Working	43.2	20.8	32.6	3.4	54,472	51.0
	Total	51.8	20.4	25.1	2.7	106,843	100

Source: ONS LS, author's analysis.

upward mobility from both the intermediate and working classes (roughly 50% and 65% respectively) are largely driven by the expanding 'room at the top', and the declining working class, which by 2001 was half the size it had been in 1971/81; but they do not mean that their chances are equalised with those from more privileged origins. If we look at the figures in another way we can observe that, while under a third (31.6%) of those from working-class backgrounds end up in the routine/manual classes, it is possible to calculate that they make up two thirds of those classes at 2001.[4]

Also to be noted is the class gradient in unemployment. Though not a class outcome per se, unemployment is a distinctly disadvantageous position to occupy and the risks of unemployment are not evenly distributed across occupations. Moreover, the stock of people who are measured

as unemployed at a point in time will be weighted towards the long-term unemployed, compared to the transiently unemployed.

Moving on to look at how these patterns vary with ethnic group, Table 2.6 first shows the distributions for the white non-migrant group. This compares very closely with the overall distributions, which is hardly surprising given that this group dominates the overall distributions numerically.

Table 2.7 shows the patterns of destinations according to origins for Caribbeans. This Table shows rather less retention in managerial and professional classes for those of service-class origins, in addition to the fact that service-class origins accounted for only 13% of origins, rather than the 29% for the cohort as a whole. It also shows no clear class origin gradient for unemployment – rates are high across all three origin classes; and the chances of working-class outcomes are only slightly lower for those from service-class backgrounds than for those from working-class backgrounds. Upward mobility is occurring from the working class, but, given the extremely heavy concentration in working-class

---

[4] This figure of two thirds has been calculated as 31.6% (=19,506) of 61,728, the original size of the working class, as a share of the size of the final working class which makes up 24.6% (=29,485) of 119,858, the overall total. 19,506 represents 66% (or two thirds) of 29,485.

Table 2.7: Social class destinations 2001 according to social class origins (row percentages): Caribbeans

| | | Destinations (2001) | | | | | |
		Professional/ managerial	Intermediate	Routine/ manual	Unemployed	Total (N)	Column %
Origins (1971/1981)	Service	52.5	21.2	17.5	8.8	137	12.8
	Intermediate	38.5	28.1	29.2	4.2	96	9.0
	Working	44.6	24.0	22.9	8.5	836	78.2
	Total	45.1	24.0	22.7	8.1	1,069	100

Source: ONS LS, author's analysis

Table 2.8: Social class destinations 2001 according to social class origins (row percentages): Indians

| | | Destinations (2001) | | | | | |
		Professional/ managerial	Intermediate	Routine/ manual	Unemployed	Total (N)	Column %
Origins (1971/1981)	Service	75.9	11.8	9.6	2.7	187	13.6
	Intermediate	59.6	27.9	10.4	2.2	183	13.3
	Working	55.6	19.2	21.6	3.6	1,008	73.1
	Total	58.8	19.4	18.5	3.3	1,378	100

Source: ONS LS, author's analysis

Table 2.9: Social class destinations 2001 according to social class origins (row percentages): Pakistanis

| | | Destinations (2001) | | | | | |
		Professional/ managerial	Intermediate	Routine/ manual	Unemployed/ other*	Total (N)	Column %
Origins (1971/1981)	Service	47.7	27.3	11.4	13.6	44	7.2
	Intermediate	33.3	25.3	19.2	22.2	99	16.3
	Working	30.7	20.9	21.9	26.5	465	76.5
	Total	32.4	22.0	20.7	24.8	608	100

Note: *As a result of small cell sizes, 'unemployed' had to be combined with 'other' for this table, which means this column and the overall row percentages are not directly comparable with the preceding ones. In order to provide a direct point of comparison between the other ethnic groups and the Pakistanis, versions of Tables 2.5, 2.6, 2.7, 2.8 and 2.10 that aggregate 'unemployed' and 'other' (as in this Table) are included in the Technical Appendix (available at www.jrf.org.uk/bookshop).
Source: ONS LS, author's analysis

origins of over 75% (a factor consistent with downward mobility or limited opportunities for the migrant generation), a greater level of upward mobility might be expected. This point is illustrated in more detail in Table 2.11 below.

Table 2.8 shows the pattern of transitions for Indians. Here, despite levels of service-class origins comparable to the Caribbean group, the table shows an even higher level of retention in the managerial and professional classes among those who had service-class origins, than for the white non-migrants. There are also higher levels of upward mobility from the working and intermediate social classes, as might be expected given that nearly three quarters of origins were in the working class. However, the levels of upward mobility are such that higher proportions end up in the

Table 2.10: Social class destinations 2001 according to social class origins (row percentages): white migrants

		Destinations (2001)					
		Professional/ managerial	Intermediate	Routine/ manual	Unemployed	Total (N)	Column %
Origins (1971/1981)	Service	68.8	18.0	9.6	3.6	532	18.6
	Intermediate	57.6	22.1	17.2	3.1	542	18.9
	Working	49.9	22.3	23.8	4.0	1,793	62.5
	Total	54.9	21.5	19.9	3.8	2,867	100

Source: ONS LS, author's analysis

managerial professional classes in 2001 than from the white non-migrant group.

Table 2.9 shows Pakistanis' origin to destination transitions. The pattern here is comparable to that of the Caribbeans, but showing apparently even less retention in the professional/managerial classes for those from service-class origins, despite an even smaller proportion starting off in the service-class. There is also – apparently – less upward mobility from the routine and working classes, resulting in the lowest proportions in the professional/managerial classes in 2001 of any of the groups considered. However, the small numbers in this group resulted in the need to aggregate the 'unemployed' and 'other' categories to avoid small cell sizes. This means that it is not directly comparable with the preceding tables in that the proportions in the unemployed/other column are relatively inflated and the proportions in the other cells correspondingly deflated.

Finally, Table 2.10 shows the transitions for the white migrants. The patterns here are, at first sight, very similar to those for the white non-migrants, but while they show just as high levels of retention in the professional/managerial classes for those from service-class origins, they also reveal higher overall unemployment rates and no apparent gradient in unemployment. Substantial upward mobility rates have, on the other hand, resulted in higher proportions ending up in the professional and managerial classes despite far smaller proportions starting off here.

To summarise these findings in graphical form, and focusing now only on the class transitions (that is, excluding unemployment as an outcome), Figure 2.2 shows the proportions in different destinations according to their starting positions.

The three column percentages across each ethnic group sum to 100%, and each section of the column represents the share of each group that comes from a particular origin for each destination. It clearly illustrates the impact of 'more room at the top' on the minority groups – but also shows differences between them. Thus, nearly 40% of Caribbeans (excluding those who end up unemployed) come from working-class origins but end in up in the professional/managerial classes. This is in large part a consequence of the fact that nearly 80% of them started off in the working class. Thus we can see that a further 20% of them had both origins and destinations in the working class. By contrast, the Indians started off with a slightly lower proportion having working-class origins, but a higher proportion of these – and over 40% of the whole group – ended up with professional/managerial destinations from working-class origins. Only around 16% of the Indians from working-class origins were retained in routine/manual occupations from working-class origins. The Pakistanis diverge from the Caribbeans in the opposite direction: with only a slightly smaller proportion (around 75%) starting off in the working class, less than a third of this group manages to move from working-class origins to professional/managerial destinations.

Figure 2.3 shows, by contrast, the composition of the destination classes for the different groups. Again, the three column percentages across each ethnic group sum to 100%, and here each section of the column represents the share of each group that ends up in a particular destination from each origin. It illustrates how the composition of the professional managerial classes is dominated by those from the working class, particularly for the Indians, where this destination is more common than for any other group. For the white non-migrants, while the increased size of this

Figure 2.2: Percentages from different ethnic groups ending up in particular class destinations, by their class origins

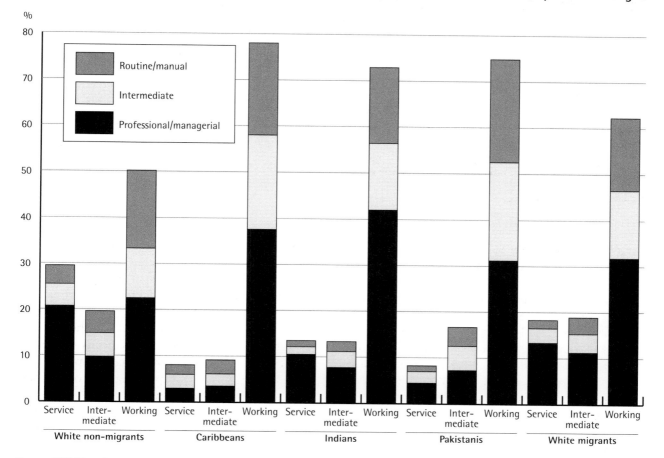

Source: ONS LS, author's analysis

professional/managerial class means that those with service-class origins only make up under half of it, those with such origins make up a much smaller share of the other two classes: around a quarter of the intermediate class and less than a fifth of the working class. This illustrates the power of class retention – or the crude impact of origins on destinations, an impact which I go on to unpick further in Chapter 3.

Summary of ethnic groups' social mobility

It is also possible to summarise the total levels of mobility experienced by the different groups and to break that down into upward and downward mobility. Table 2.11 provides such a summary. Upward mobility is measured as the moves from working-class origins to intermediate and professional/managerial class destinations, and from intermediate to professional/managerial; and downward mobility is measured as moves from service-class origins to any other destination than

professional/managerial, from intermediate to working class and unemployment and from working class to unemployment.[5]

Table 2.11 clearly shows the high levels of upward mobility among the minority groups (except the Pakistanis) relative to the white group. It also shows that in the region of 70% of Indians, Caribbeans, white migrants and white non-migrants experience a move in some direction between their origin and their destination class. However, referring back to the earlier point about the impact of structural changes in class distributions on absolute mobility, combined with the striking preponderance of minority group members' origins in the working class, reasonably high levels of upward mobility are only to be expected for the minority groups. The reasonably high levels of downward mobility within the Caribbean and white migrant groups are, in this context, especially striking, given the limited possibilities for progressing further down the class

---

[5] For the purposes of this illustration, unemployment has been incorporated at the bottom of the class hierarchy as it plays an important part in the story for some groups.

Figure 2.3: The composition of 2001 class positions according to parental social class origins, by ethnic group

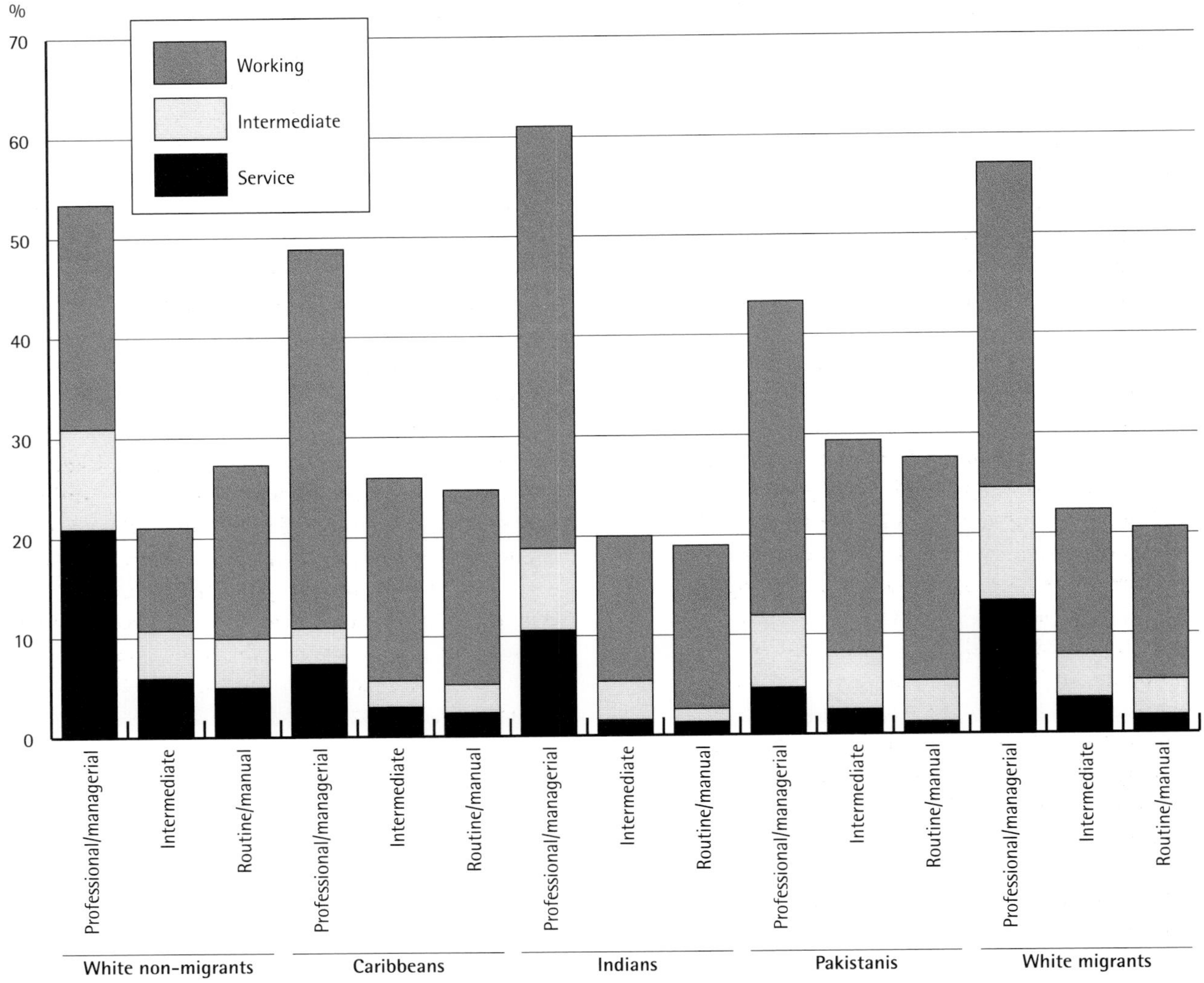

Source: ONS LS, author's analysis

Table 2.11: Upward and downward mobility by ethnic group and mobility implied by changing class structure alone

	White non-migrant	Caribbean	Indian	Pakistani*	White migrant
Upward mobility	42.3	57.1	62.7	44.9	56.0
Downward mobility	15.7	15.4	7.6	Suppressed	12.2
Immobility	42.0	27.5	29.7	Suppressed	31.8
Net gain, i.e. upward mobility minus downward mobility	26.6	41.7	55.1	Suppressed	43.8
Net upward mobility needed to achieve 2001 class distributions across ethnic groups	20.8	48.0	42.9	46.3	32.3
Difference between actual and minimum upward mobility	5.8	−6.3	12.2	Suppressed	11.5

Note: *The different construction of the transition table for the Pakistanis, resulting from the need to suppress potentially disclosive data by aggregating the 'unemployed' and 'other' categories, also has implications for this table: the cells indicated could only be calculated precisely if 'unemployed' and 'other' were disaggregated.

Source: ONS LS, author's analysis

hierarchy – except into unemployment. The net gain (that is, upward mobility minus downward mobility) is therefore also calculated. This is one measure of ethnic minorities' success in the British labour market. However, if we take seriously their disadvantaged position in the parents' generation and assume that some of this 'success' should be seen more as compensation for limited opportunities in the migrant generation, we might want to modify such claims – and modify them by looking at what levels of upward mobility would be required to ensure parity in the class structure.

To develop this point further, it is possible to calculate the *minimum* upward (and downward, into unemployment) mobility that would be required for each group to mimic the overall destination patterns found in Table 2.5 for the whole cohort, that is, for all groups to have 52% in the professional/managerial classes, 20.4% in the intermediate classes, 24.6% in the working class and 2.8% unemployed. To achieve these distributions, that is to achieve ethnic even if not social class equality, and with the minimum of cross-class transitions, would require only 23.6% upward mobility for the white group (the percentage change needed in the professional and intermediate classes to match the 2001 distribution) but 35.1% for the white migrant group, 45.7% for the Indians, 49.1% for the Pakistanis and 50.8% for the Caribbeans, whose origins were most heavily concentrated in the working class.

Table 2.11 shows the net upward mobility 'required', that is these levels of upward mobility minus the 2.8% downward mobility into unemployment. If we subtract these net minimum levels of upward mobility required to achieve ethnic equality from the net actual upward mobility, we can see that the minority groups' 'success' becomes less striking. It is still notable for the Indians and white migrants compared to the white non-migrants, but for Caribbeans and clearly for Pakistanis (although small cell sizes do not permit the exact calculations to be recorded for the latter), the levels of upward mobility are lower than the demands of a simple notion of equality of outcomes across groups would require.

In the next chapter I go on from these explorations of overall mobility transitions to investigate further the question of differential outcomes and whether, and to what extent, study members' class outcomes may be related to their origins – their parents' characteristics – as well as to their own educational achievements, and whether differences can be observed across the ethnic groups once these factors are taken into account.

3

Explaining social class outcomes

In this chapter I consider the role of class background alongside other background characteristics and the sample members' own educational achievement in contributing to the distinctive patterns of intergenerational mobility revealed in the previous chapter. I also consider what religion can add to our understanding of patterns of social mobility. In doing this, this chapter raises the question of whether the differences by ethnic group can be ascribed to an 'ethnic' effect per se or can be accounted for by variations in other characteristics that are associated with different ethnic groups. In particular, this chapter explores the ability of educational achievement to mediate first generation class disadvantage and to account for the upward mobility of minority ethnic groups.

The analysis and discussion builds on the more general concern in the mobility literature with the relationships between origins, education and destinations (see, for example, Halsey et al, 1980; Breen and Whelan, 1993; Goldthorpe, 1997; Breen, 1998) and on the specific emphasis in Heath's work in relation to understanding the role of education in differential ethnic group outcomes (Cheng and Heath, 1993; Heath and McMahon, 1997, 2005). It has been regularly observed that levels of educational achievement vary widely between ethnic groups (for example, Modood, 1997b, 2003; National Statistics, 2004). While it does not diminish the importance of absolute differences in class mobility between groups if education is found to have a substantial role in explaining them, it does clarify some of the processes and favour certain explanatory accounts. It indicates that policy attention might be most valuably focused on the education – and educational experiences – of different groups to ensure greater parity of outcomes. Heath and McMahon (2005) found, moreover, that even when education was taken into account in measuring mobility, an ethnic group effect (or 'penalty') remained for certain groups. It is instructive to explore

whether this is also shown with these data and the somewhat different design and premises of this study.

Educational levels of parents have also been shown to be important in facilitating the upward mobility or higher class retention of their children. Parental educational qualifications can also stand in for some sort of latent class position that may have been disguised by downward occupational mobility for the parents on migration. Parental education is therefore included alongside parental class and two indicators of economic status in the household of origin – car ownership and housing tenure – to investigate the ways in which parents' capital (human and economic) is related to their children's outcomes. As each parent's educational level may be independently important, both are included separately. This means that this variable also includes the possibility that there is no co-resident father/mother to have an educational level. Thus, these variables also incorporate family structure. The information on qualifications for 1971 and 1981 is limited by the form of the question asked in those censuses. The parental educational variable derived from these can only distinguish higher qualifications levels, which were held by only a small minority of the population in this period (only 9% of the sample mothers and 15% of the sample fathers had such qualifications). There is no way of distinguishing between those parents with no qualifications at all and those with some non-advanced qualifications. This is aside from the important issue of comparability of qualifications across minority groups, and the extent to which variation in the meaning or exchange value of qualifications obtained in different countries or different types of institution may influence observed patterns and relationships.

Area effects are also potentially important in influencing outcomes in the second generation. There are two issues here. First, there is the extent to which certain minority groups may be concentrated in areas that suffer from processes of deindustrialisation and the consequently more limited employment opportunities. While it has been argued that minority ethnic group members have adapted relatively well to deindustrialisation (Iganski and Payne, 1999), it remains the case that minority groups are still heavily concentrated in some of the most deprived areas with the consequent impacts on life chances that have been stressed in discussions of social exclusion. The second way in which area may be important is that concentrations of the same ethnic group have been argued to be potential resources. Ethnic group concentrations in particular areas, may, it is argued, enhance social capital, enable some pooling of resources and capital and aid enterprise.

Borjas (1992) developed the concept of effective 'ethnic capital' to encapsulate the possibilities that geographical proximity of people both from the same ethnic group and from other minority ethnic groups might bring. On the other hand, the distinction within the social capital literature between bridging and bonding social capital (Putnam, 2000), has highlighted the extent to which the positive aspects of geographical concentrations may at the same time inhibit wider advancement: the groups may bond, but not be able to build bridges to other social networks. Work by Dorsett (1998) in the British context has shown that, while for some groups geographical concentration and concentration in disadvantaged areas can be seen to go hand in hand, those minority group members who are successful may also elect for geographical proximity. For example, some Indians have moved into particular London suburbs where relative concentration can provide them with cultural resources, which are independent of, or go alongside, their success. This option of combining concentration and cultural resources with moves to relatively affluent areas is likely to be possible only within London, however.

The role of geography is, therefore, layered and complex. In this study, an attempt has been made to capture some form of area effect through the use of a variable summarising the level of minority group concentration in the ward of origin. This variable aggregates minority ethnic groups since the area group variable did not enable the individual groups considered in this study – and therefore 'own' group – to be distinguished. However, to the extent that areas with higher proportions from minority ethnic groups are distinctive, this variable may reveal something about area effects.

A final issue that is explored in this chapter is the role of religion – or rather, how it can modify our understanding of ethnic group effects. When trying to explain different outcomes according to ethnic group and, in particular, when focusing on the great disadvantage experienced by Pakistani and Bangladeshi minority groups, some (for example, Modood, 1997c) have suggested that the reason an ethnic penalty cannot be observed to operate *consistently* across minority groups (there is plenty of evidence that it operates, as discussed in Chapter 1), is because the 'ethnic penalty' is, rather, a 'religious penalty'. Islam is, by this explanation, seen as the principal object of discrimination, rather than any minority ethnicity; and differences in experiences between groups are better understood in relation to the histories and trajectories of ethno-religious groups than 'simply' in relation to ethnicity. There are problems of interpretation in relation to differentiating by religion (as much as or more so than for ethnicity) in terms of the causal processes invoked and how they are associated with religious groups. Nevertheless, the inclusion of a religion question in the 2001 Census gives the possibility of exploring further how religious affiliation is associated with the patterning of social mobility. This chapter therefore considers what associations religion has with particular patterns of social class outcomes, and how including religion in the analysis can refine our understanding of ethnic group processes.

Achieving higher social class outcomes

Individuals' chances of ending up in the professional or managerial class were calculated holding an increasing succession of factors constant. The results of these nested models exploring the effect of different factors on probabilities of class 'success' can be found in Table A1 in the Appendix. The main results from them are summarised and illustrated here. The effects of origin class and minority group concentration in the ward in which they were living in 1971/81 were examined, alongside sex, age, cohort and partnership status of the sample member, as the starting point for looking at the relationship between origins and destinations (Model 1). Rather than testing how far ethnic differences in achievement of social class position might be mediated by origins, the order in which different characteristics were added in was designed to identify general patterns of the impact of origins on destinations and then to explore whether these were mediated by or differed according to ethnic group. Successively, origin economic variables and parental qualifications were included (Model 2), followed by the effect of ethnicity over and above these origins (Model 3), then the sample members' own educational qualifications (Model 4), and finally some indicators of respondent's economic status (car ownership and housing tenure) (Model 5). The economic status variables were included as the final stage with some caution, as they are likely to be outcomes of destination class status rather than mediating or independent effects. They are therefore not extensively discussed, but this final set of potential contributory factors is provided to consider whether influencing the achievement of a successful class position can be distinguished from the implied economic gains of such a position.

When we just look at the effects of the first set of variables, we find a clear effect of origins on destinations. Those from service-class origins were three times as likely as their counterparts from working-class occupations to end up in a professional or managerial class, and those from intermediate-class occupations were 28% more likely. And this is the case when sex, age, cohort, marital (partnership) status and area composition at origin were held constant. Sex had no significant independent effect on chances of success, which is perhaps unsurprising given that the outcome class is based on a family class taking account of both partners' occupations. Any sex difference would, therefore, effectively apply to only single men and women. Also, as a result of the way destination class is measured by taking the higher class of the two partners, it is unsurprising to find that partnership has a strong influence on probability of ending up in a professional/managerial occupation. It has also been suggested that potential to partner is, itself, an indication of latent characteristics that might make occupational success more obtainable – but such an explanation is unnecessary to explain the effect demonstrated here.

Interestingly we find that, controlling for cohort, which is itself insignificant, it is the younger age groups who are more likely to achieve a professional/managerial class position. The implication could be that it is the younger age groups who are more likely to obtain the qualifications necessary to obtaining managerial and professional positions. This hypothesis is supported by Model 4, where, controlling for education,

younger age groups become *less* likely to achieve a professional/managerial position.

The area variables show that any concentration of minorities in the ward of origin greater than 0% makes a professional/managerial class outcome more likely, although there is not any clear pattern with the increasing levels of concentration. It suggests that, instead of there being something in the concentration of ethnic minorities, it is the wards with no minority group presence at all which are distinct. Possibly such areas tended to be the least economically dynamic and thus failed to attract any inward migration up to the early 1980s; or it is possible that they allowed less scope for upward mobility. While the exact size of these effects varies according to the range of characteristics taken account of, the positive impact remains and even increases as other factors are taken into account.

The second model, where parents' qualifications and origin household economic status are added in, shows that parental social class has an independent effect from other parental characteristics – education and economic resources. Conversely, controlling for class, mother's and father's qualifications both increase the chance of their child having a professional/managerial qualification, as do the economic status variables. Including these variables reduces the impact of service-class origins – but does not remove it. Thus, while some of the advantage of service-class origins clearly comes through the power of economic resources and perhaps through the educational support and motivation provided by highly educated parents, there are other aspects to class advantage which cannot be explained in this way. We can think, perhaps, of networks and the social or cultural capital that more privileged origins may provide access to (Bourdieu, 1997).

Interestingly, while lacking a mother inhibits chances of professional/managerial class destinations relative to having a mother with no or lower qualifications (as might be expected), lacking a father increases the chances of professional/managerial class destinations relative to having an unqualified (or at least not highly qualified) father. While the former result draws attention to the importance of mothers in developing their children's skills and education, it is difficult to know how to account for this latter result. It may be that in such fatherless households aspirations are particularly high, or that they are distinctive in terms of family structure (in ways that are not measured, such as number of siblings), which relatively facilitates upward mobility. An alternative explanation is that unqualified/ lower qualified fathers have a positively restricting effect that is absent when they are not there. Moreover, by definition, we do not know the characteristics of absent fathers. They are likely to be a combination of both the more and the less advantaged, and their absence may have less impact on the suppressing of successful outcomes than the advantages that at least some of them offer in enabling successful outcomes. Even if non-resident, they may contribute the benefits of their economic, social and human capital assets to their children.

Finally, once parents' qualifications and economic status are taken into account the effect of cohort on profession or managerial outcomes becomes significant and is negative. This indicates that, controlling for age group, once the higher levels of qualifications that might be seen in parents in 1981 compared to those in 1971 are factored out, those from the 1981 cohort are slightly less likely to achieve a service-class origin than their counterparts from the decade earlier. That is, it suggests that the 10 more years that the older cohort has accumulated constitutes a slight advantage in terms of class position, and one which is not outweighed by the potentially lower levels of educational achievement that the older cohort might be expected to have acquired with the general rise in levels of qualifications over time.

It was only after establishing these patterns of the relationship between various characteristics of the parents and their children's outcomes that ethnic group was examined in addition (Model 3). Here, whether there was any distinct impact of ethnic group once background had been taken into account was being tested. This model was thus engaging with one of the recurrent claims in the literature that differential ethnic group success in the second generation can be linked to parents' characteristics and the availability of different 'capitals'. The absence of ethnic group effects would not imply that life chances were the same for all ethnic groups; but it would suggest that it was parents' achieved occupation on migration, combined with the resources (human and economic capital) that the migrant generation brought with them that determine the very different outcomes we observe for the different groups today, and that common processes post-migration might be assumed to operate in England and Wales. This

would indicate that a focus on class inequalities rather than ethnic group might be most appropriate for preventing the transmission of disadvantage into subsequent generations. What we find, instead, is that all the minority groups except the Pakistanis (and the Bangladeshis – but the result for that group is not statistically significant) have a higher probability of professional/managerial outcomes than can be explained by their origins (as imperfectly measured here) alone.

This is congruent with the very high proportions with working-class origins shown in the preceding chapter that might make us anticipate greater levels of achievement from working-class backgrounds. It would also support the idea, discussed in Chapter 1, that these groups may have experienced downward mobility on migration and that this was not the experience of the Pakistanis (Daniel, 1968; Smith, 1977; Modood, 1997b). Nevertheless, it is interesting to find this effect even when other factors relating to origins (parental qualifications and economic status) have been accounted for. It might be expected that it would be the differences in these parental resources that would determine different rates of achievement between the groups. Instead, we find that, even controlling for these background differences, Caribbeans have a 22% greater chance of ending up in the professional classes than otherwise comparable white non-migrants; white migrants have a 30% greater chance; and the other groups have a greater chance of between 56% (Indians) and 75% (Black Africans).

The increased chances of ending up in a professional/managerial position (comparing like with like) are perhaps not very surprising given the low starting points and some anticipation of flexibility within the class structure. However, the differences between the groups are perhaps of more interest. How is it that Black Africans manage to overcome the effects of their origins more than the other groups? And, even more strikingly, why should it be that Pakistanis, even given their working-class concentration at origin, are *less* likely to achieve professional/managerial positions than their white counterparts once their origins are controlled for? Comparable outcomes with the white group would indicate that their preponderance in the working class was related to a reasonably close match between their occupations on migration and their pre-migration skills and class. Class processes within England and Wales would then have taken over to impact on prospects for the second generation. Instead, we find a strong negative effect for this group that suggests that they have fared less well than they might have expected to do under such conditions. Furthermore, it implies a level of polarisation between minority ethnic groups, with those who are not so well placed to achieve occupational success experiencing cumulative effects of class- and ethnicity-related disadvantage.

A number of factors not measured here might help to explain this result: different family sizes at origin, so that resources are shared between a relatively large number of siblings; diversity within the working class, so that skilled occupations which might lead to better prospects for the second generation are combined with unskilled and more residual ones, and with the Pakistani migrants being possibly more grouped towards the unskilled dimension; diversity, also, within the service class, so that this broad category encompasses those at a range of different levels of job security, earnings levels and status; diversity within those parents without advanced qualifications, ranging from those with no qualifications to those with numbers of non-advanced qualifications, with the Pakistanis having more with no qualifications and the more successful groups having more with some qualifications (Platt, 2002). Different age profiles (see Technical Appendix (available at www.jrf.org.uk/bookshop) for a further discussion of age distributions across groups) may play some role, but including both age and cohort in the model controls for such effects, with the younger cohort overall continuing to have slightly lower probabilities of professional and managerial class destinations.

Another line of explanation might be found by considering the way that class has been constructed as a family class. That is, for married or cohabiting couples it is the higher social class of either partner that determines the family class. The differential labour market participation of Pakistani women and their greater tendency to be in routine/manual occupations, would mean that for Pakistanis there was less opportunity for women to boost the 'family class', a process that might be taking place for other groups, especially between working-class husbands and intermediate-class wives. This point can be explored further by looking at the proportion of men and women from the different ethnic groups for whom family class alters their 'individual' class. Figure 3.1 shows the proportionate class change expressed as gains or

Figure 3.1: Proportionate class gains or losses from individual to family class allocation in 2001 by ethnic group: men

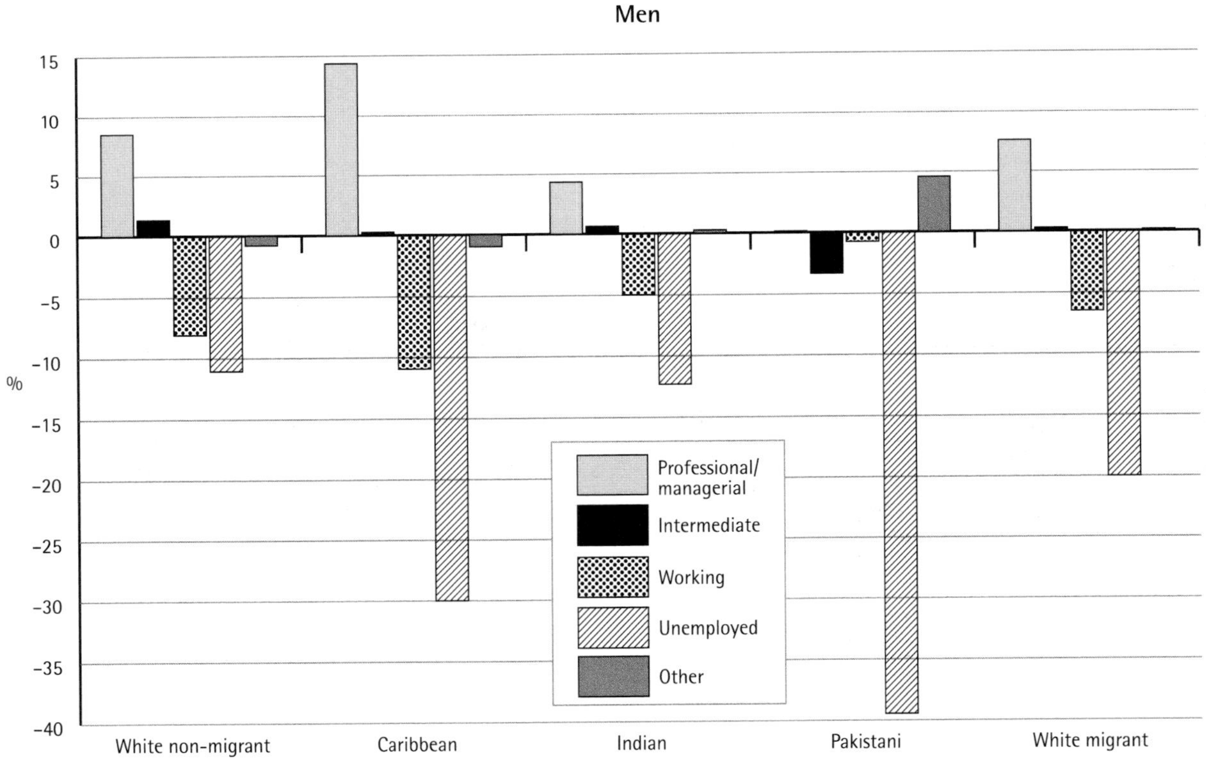

Source: ONS LS, author's analysis

losses to the different classes by adoption of a family rather than an individual class for men from the five main ethnic groups. Figure 3.2 shows the corresponding picture for women.

Figure 3.1 does indeed show that the boost to professional class share of class distribution from marriage is indeed negligible for the Pakistanis. And while marriage results in a large proportionate decrease in unemployed families, it also sees a relatively large increase in those defined as 'other'. This is the only group for which there is a proportionate increase in those classified in the 'other' following marriage (due to 'other' being the selected category if one spouse is so classified and the other has only missing information). As both the unemployed and those allocated to 'other' are very small numerically, and the whole ethnic group consists of fewer than 300 people, the proportionate contribution can be affected by small changes in numbers.

For Caribbean men, we can see that marriage boosts their class profile, with the share allocated to the professional class increasing by some 14% (from around 30% of the distribution to around 44%) by taking family class as the outcome measure rather than individual class.

Figure 3.2 illustrates the comparable impact on using family class for women. It shows how family class brings a substantial boost to professional class distributions for women from all groups – although somewhat less so for Pakistani and Caribbean women.

One final point for consideration with regard to the strong, negative effect for Pakistanis in relation to higher class outcomes is the suggestion that the 'rewards' for Muslim women from education and assets at origin might be in marriage itself, rather than in occupational mobility, thereby reducing their tendency to be upwardly mobile. However, even if these potential factors play some role the Pakistani effect remains noteworthy, and persists even when the educational achievement of the children themselves is taken account of, as discussed further later in the chapter.

The next step was to consider the educational level of the sample members themselves and how this might modify both the impact of origins (that is, advantaged parents enabling their children through education) or ethnicity (that is, minority groups gaining their upward mobility, and greater parity, through education). Unsurprisingly, increasing levels of education are strongly associated with higher

Figure 3.2: Proportionate class gains or losses from individual to family class allocation in 2001 by ethnic group: women

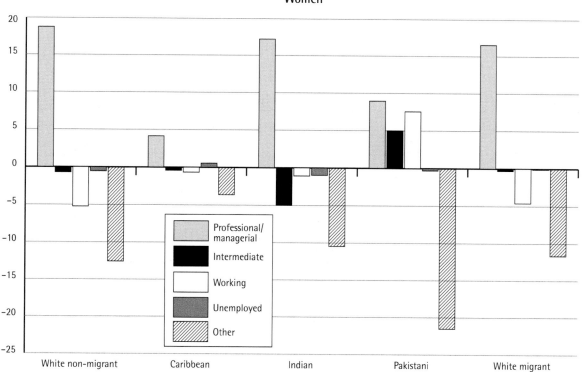

Source: ONS LS, author's analysis

probabilities of professional/managerial destinations, and the impact of origins is correspondingly reduced. Privileged and more educated groups gain advantage for the next generation through ensuring that their children gain educational qualifications – an aspect of class mobility that has long been noted (Glass, 1954; Halsey et al, 1980). But the origin effects, though reduced, do not disappear. Thus parents' capitals continue to play an important role in their children's achievement of professional and managerial positions, over and above the educational gains that these resources may help the children to achieve.

It is interesting to note that it is only once education is included that a significant effect for sex appears. As mentioned above, the sex variable will primarily be picking up the differences between single men and women, but its small positive value once education is held constant indicates that men have a small advantage over women of the same educational level in gaining a higher social class position. The reason the effect could not be seen before education was held constant can be explained by the fact that the (single) women in the sample are slightly better educated than the (single) men, and therefore they achieve a comparable class position through higher levels of education.

Turning to the ethnic group effects, we find that once education is held constant the positive ethnic group effects disappear. That is, the greater chances of access to professional/managerial destinations than their parental class origins would imply, which were observed before controlling for education, would appear to be achieved through education. The argument that upward mobility is achieved through education for some groups is then supported by this finding for all groups except the Pakistanis and Bangladeshis.

When educational qualifications are held constant there is a further reduction in the relative chances of occupational success for Pakistanis, and Bangladeshis show a similar disadvantage. Education serves to increase chances of professional or managerial class outcomes across the sample. But for these two groups, education is not able to compensate for whatever it is about, or associated with, Pakistani or Bangladeshi ethnicity that results in relative disadvantage. Lower levels of educational success are not able to explain lower chances of professional or managerial class outcomes for these two groups; and they are not achieving the levels

of occupational success that not only their origins but also their educational achievements should imply. This is a startling finding, even given the earlier attempts to explain relative Pakistani disadvantage. There seems no obvious explanation for why Pakistanis' and Bangladeshis' education does not at least reduce the impact of ethnicity. Given the important role of education as a route to success, the reasons why it does not 'work' for Pakistanis and Bangladeshis, or why it is not used in the same way, warrants further explanation.[6] There may be geographical factors that are not being captured by the area ethnic concentration variable, but it seems unlikely that such additional geographical factors could fully account for this finding.

It was in an attempt to investigate this result further that the final model (Model 5) was run, which included as potential explanatory characteristics the sample members' own household car ownership and housing tenure. As noted above, including these as potential contributory factors to professional/managerial destinations is slightly problematic as greater income and associated living standards, which are proxied by these two variables, are likely to stem from, as much as contribute to, higher social class position. However, it seemed important to ascertain whether lack of assets in the current generation could help to explain the failure to translate educational success into achieved class position. When these economic variables were added in, the parental economic variables reduced in size, as might be expected, with some of the wealth achieving its effect on destinations by being passed on to the children But they still retained a significant, if smaller, positive impact on higher class outcomes. However, while inclusion of these variables rendered the Bangladeshis' reduced chances of professional or managerial outcomes no longer significantly different from the white non-migrants' (perhaps due to the small numbers of Bangladeshis in the sample), the probability of professional or managerial outcomes for the Pakistanis reduced still further relative to white non-migrants with otherwise comparable characteristics. With all these characteristics held constant, Pakistanis had a 60%

---

[6] Most of the differentiation between 2001 educational levels is between the lower levels with A-levels and above being aggregated, so the fact that there are substantial differences in tertiary education and how it translates into occupational success for different ethnic groups is unlikely to contribute to this effect.

Figure 3.3: The proportion from each group predicted to be in professional/managerial class (95% confidence intervals given in brackets)

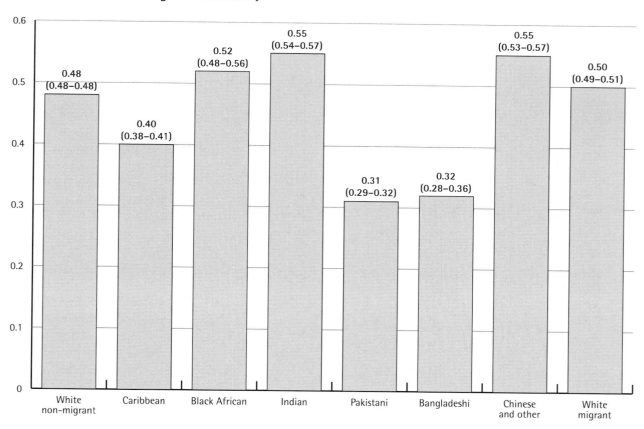

Source: ONS LS, author's analysis

lower chance of professional or managerial outcomes compared to their white non-migrant counterparts. Pakistanis are clearly disadvantaged relative to other groups in terms of achievement of higher class positions not only compared to those with similar origins, but also compared to those of the same educational level and with similar economic assets.

Given that the inclusion of sample members' own economic status variables did not help us to understand the Pakistani disadvantage, and given the problems of negative causation (identified earlier) from the inclusion of such variables in an attempt to account for social class outcomes, The remainder of this chapter, with its further exploration of issues raised by the differences in class outcomes and the contribution of different factors, will exclude these variables. The set of characteristics that subsequent models will hold constant when developing this analysis and exploring further the effect of ethnicity (and religion) on outcomes, will, therefore, be: parents' social class and qualifications, household economic status at origin, area minority ethnic concentration,

cohort, and study members' own age, marital status, sex, and highest educational qualifications.

Figure 3.3 shows the predicted probabilities of being in the professional/managerial classes by ethnic group estimated taking the above set of characteristics into account, but based on the effects associated with group members' actual characteristics. It shows the very low probability of a 'successful' outcome for Pakistanis and Bangladeshis, and the high probability for Indians, the mixed 'Chinese and other' group and the white migrants. The 95% confidence intervals shown on the figure indicate that none of the predicted probabilities for these particular minority groups overlap with those for the white non-migrant group, indicating genuine differences in chances.

If these then are the overall predicted chances for the different groups, how much is determined by the groups' characteristics (for example, different backgrounds and different levels of educational achievement) and how much is determined by an 'ethnicity effect'? After all, as Figure 3.4 shows, the probabilities vary with class background, and we

Figure 3.4: The proportion from each class of origin predicted to be in professional/managerial class, by sex

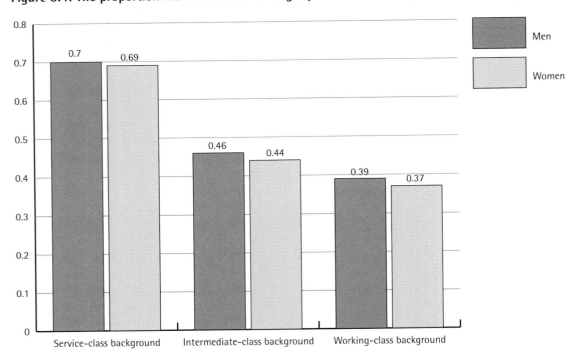

Source: ONS LS, author's analysis

saw in Chapter 2 how class background varied by group.

One way of looking at this is to investigate what the predicted probabilities would be if the group members retained their characteristics but were attributed the ethnic group effect from a different group. Figure 3.5, shows the predictions for men of working-class origins from a selection of groups dependent upon having either the white non-migrant or the Pakistani ethnicity effect attributed to them. In the figure, the impact of being white non-migrant or Pakistani has been applied to the members of a set of ethnic groups. Thus, the white non-migrants with the white non-migrant effect and the Pakistanis with the Pakistani chances are the actual predicted probabilities of ending up in professional or managerial occupations for men of working-class origins from these two groups, 0.38 and 0.24 respectively. The remaining predictions are 'what ifs'. Figure 3.5 shows that if all groups had their own characteristics but the ethnic group effect of being white non-migrant, the Indian men from working-class backgrounds would come out ahead on the strength of their other characteristics. However, the Pakistanis would also do substantially (and, as the 95% confidence intervals show, significantly) better than their white non-migrant peers from working-class backgrounds. They should clearly be achieving higher levels of occupational

success than they are, with all the implications that follow from that. In normalising Indian 'success' and Pakistani 'disadvantage', research has tended to look for particular characteristics (especially background or educational qualifications) to explain the big differences between their outcomes. This analysis suggests, however, that it is not only or even predominantly such characteristics, in so far as they are successfully captured here, that are leading to Pakistanis' disadvantage. Instead we need to look further than is possible in this study to shed more light on this finding, including taking account of more aspects of potentially measurable variation between groups.

The following sections of this chapter develop the analysis in a number of ways. First, I briefly explore whether there are any interaction effects. That is, I examine whether the impact of certain characteristics is different for different sub-groups, for example, whether the impact of origins on destinations is different for men than for women. Second, I consider all possible class outcomes simultaneously, rather than just achievement of professional/managerial class compared to all other outcomes. And third, I investigate what religion can add to our understanding of ethnic group differences in social mobility.

Figure 3.5: The proportion of men from working-class origins from a selection of ethnic groups predicted to be in professional/managerial class, with alternative ethnic group effects (95% confidence intervals given in brackets)

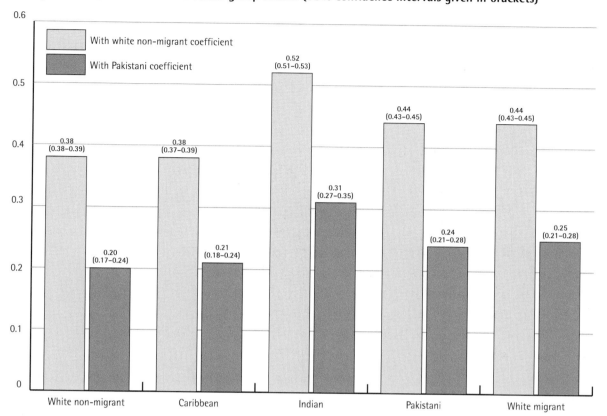

Source: ONS LS, author's analysis

Interaction effects

Here I briefly examine whether there is any evidence that the impact of social class origins shows distinctive patterns according to sex or ethnic group, as might be anticipated. There has, for example, been much discussion of the different occupational and educational profiles of Caribbean men and women (for example, Modood 1997a, 1997b). Caribbean women are also more likely to form their own households, even when they have children, than women from other groups. Might it be therefore that any ethnic group effects are distinct for men and women, with men potentially not benefiting from comparable levels of moves into the professional and managerial classes once their origins are controlled for? On the other hand, the heavy concentration of minority group origins in the working class might lead us to anticipate that the relationships between origins and destinations would vary by ethnic group.

In fact, analysis does not support the hypothesis of interactions between sex and ethnic group. However, when ethnic group and class of origin are interacted some significant results are found. These

indicate that advantaged origins are of no benefit to the Caribbeans: a specific negative effect of service-class origins for Caribbeans combined with an overall positive impact of service-class origins across the sample effectively cancel each other out, indicating that for Caribbeans, unlike for most other groups, service-class origins in themselves offer no particular advantage in achieving higher social class positions. Indeed, they seem to constitute a disadvantage, if anything. This is consistent with the lack of a protective effect of class for Caribbeans found in Platt (2005), but is striking nonetheless, given that in the current study far more potentially relevant factors have been controlled for. It may be explained in part by the fact that, for Caribbeans, women's occupations play a much more significant role in determining class across couples; and yet such women's occupations are likely to fall in particular areas of the service-class (such as nursing) that offer more limited forms of the rewards typically associated with such class origins (earnings, status and so on), which are used to assist the success of the next generation.

A similar effect is found for the white migrant group, although in this case the net influence of service-class origins on higher social class outcomes was minimal rather than negative. The only other significant interaction was a very strong negative effect for Bangladeshis from intermediate-class origins. This indicates that Bangladeshis from intermediate-class origins are much less likely to end up in professional/managerial destinations than those from working-class origins. While a sizeable as well as a significant effect, the numbers of cases on which this result is based are necessarily very small for this group.

Examining all destinations

So far the analysis has looked only at comparative 'success' as measured through achievement of a professional/managerial class destination as compared with any other destination. However, there may well be differences in the probabilities of different destinations. In particular, as indicated in the previous chapter, success may be tempered by differential unemployment risks. For the next analysis, therefore, the chances of all five possible destinations (professional/managerial, intermediate, routine/manual, unemployment and other) were estimated simultaneously. To do this, the core set of variables identified above continue to be used as controls. Do we find a greater range of specific ethnic group effects if we examine all possible outcomes rather than simply the chances of professional/managerial class outcomes?

The results of this analysis are reported in Table A2 in the Appendix.[7] Here, salient aspects of those results are drawn out.

As when investigating simply the chances of professional/managerial class destinations, once a range of relevant characteristics are controlled, there remain few statistically significant specifically 'ethnic group' effects. However, those that do appear merit discussion. First is the greater propensity of Caribbeans to end up in the intermediate class, and, more particularly, unemployment, compared to their white non-migrant counterparts. The relative risks of unemployment (as an alternative to professional or managerial class destinations) are 74% higher for Caribbeans than they are for white non-migrants.

This demonstrates the importance of considering unemployment as a potential outcome alongside class destinations when examining ethnic group differences in mobility. And it is important to remember that these increased risks of unemployment are over and above the effects of age, level of qualifications, and so on. Unemployment is also a much greater risk for Bangladeshis: they are over four times as likely as white non-migrants to face unemployment compared with facing service-class outcomes, other things being equal.

Another interesting effect is the greater risk of unemployment associated with youth. This can be found both in the difference between the younger and older cohorts and, within cohorts, between the younger and older age groups. It is also worth noting the importance of service-class origins in protecting against unemployment. The greater risk for men of unemployment and the lower risk of 'other' outcomes is not surprising, particularly since, other than students, the bulk of the 'others' are lone parents, most of whom will be women. There is also a relationship between 'other' origins and both unemployment and 'other' destinations, which is intriguing. Given that 'other' is a residual category rather than a class in itself, it is perhaps surprising that it apparently transmits its effects across the generations. This tells us that coming from an unstable, unemployed or unclassifiable background has the power to reduce opportunities for the next generation.

The positive impact on better outcomes from having an absent father remains, and remains perplexing, despite the earlier attempt to account for its positive influence. Having no father present at origins renders both unemployment and manual/routine outcomes relative to professional/managerial outcomes more likely than for those with an unqualified or lower qualified father. Why this should be runs counter to established wisdom. On the other hand, having no mother present makes both unemployment and 'other' outcomes more likely.

The most striking results arise again in relation to the Pakistanis. Controlling for characteristics, they are more likely than their white non-migrant counterparts to fall into *all* other destinations compared to the chances of being in the professional/managerial classes: and they are over five times as likely as white non-migrants to be unemployed relative to being in the professional/

---

[7] The justification for reporting the results of a multinomial rather than an ordered logistic regression are discussed further in the Technical Appendix (available at www.jrf.org.uk/bookshop).

managerial classes. As stressed above, this is comparing those with similar origins, parental capital and qualifications levels. This would seem to be evidence of a group-specific disadvantage that a changing class structure and weakening of class-based intergenerational privilege is unlikely to affect.

Given that the characteristics of the different groups do in fact vary, it is instructive to ascertain what the importance of this effect is compared to the group characteristics in determining the poorer outcomes of Pakistanis overall. This can be done by applying the impact of being in a particular group to other groups, but otherwise retaining the individuals' characteristics, as was done for the previous analysis and illustrated in Figure 3.5. Both the white non-migrant and the Pakistani effects on chances of having routine/manual outcomes relative to having professional/managerial outcomes were applied to a number of groups.

The result of calculating such differential chances are illustrated, in Table 3.1, for men from four groups and looking separately at those from working-class and service-class origins. This table illustrates the impact of ethnicity on the relative risks of ending up in the routine and manual classes. The characteristics of the (male) members of the different groups are retained and the chances of this outcome associated with those characteristics. But the two ethnic group effects are applied in turn to produce the results in the first (white non-migrant) and second (Pakistani) parts of the table. Thus, the chances for white non-migrants in the first half of the table and for Pakistanis in the second half of the table are their actual predicted relative risks, while those for the other cells are their chances 'as if' they came from a different group (similar to Figure 3.5, earlier). Risks above

one show an increased risk of the working-class outcome and those below one show a reduced risk. From this we find that white non-migrants from working-class origins are only 82% as likely to end up in the working class as the professional / managerial class, and the risks for those from service-class origins (along with all the other characteristics that tend to go with such origins), are 85% less likely to end up in the professional/ managerial classes. If those from working class backgrounds had the 'Pakistani effect', however, their risks of ending up in the working class would rise to being nearly 1.5:1.

What the first half of this table shows is that Pakistanis from both service- and working-class origins would be expected to have a *lower* concentration in the working class than white non-migrants if they did not have an ethnic group effect. The relative risks for the Caribbeans and the Bangladeshis show that this is not *necessarily* the case for all ethnic groups: service-class origin Caribbeans would have a higher risk of working-class destinations than whites on the basis of their characteristics, although working-class origin Caribbeans would have a lower risk; and Bangladeshi characteristics would mean greater risks of working-class destinations than whites for both origins, even if there was no separate ethnic group effect.

The second part of the table confirms this picture by showing how the greater risks of working-class destinations associated with the Pakistani ethnic group would affect men from all groups on the basis of their other characteristics but as if they were Pakistani. It reiterates the picture given in Figure 3.5. From this we can see that whites of working-class origin would actually have a greater risk of a working-class rather than a service-class

Table 3.1: Relative risks of working class rather than professional/managerial class outcome according to own characteristics and varying ethnic group coefficient

	From working-class origin	From service-class origin
For white non-migrants based on own coefficient	0.820	0.145
For Pakistanis based on white non-migrant coefficient	0.577	0.104
Caribbean based on white non-migrant coefficient	0.711	0.251
Bangladeshis based on white non-migrant coefficient	0.828	0.188
For white non-migrants based on Pakistani coefficient	1.492	0.263
For Pakistanis based on own coefficient	1.050	0.189
Caribbeans based on Pakistani coefficient	1.292	0.456
Bangladeshis based on Pakistani coefficient	1.506	0.341

Source: ONS LS, author's analysis

outcome if they had the Pakistani ethnic group effect, while the chances are about equal for Pakistanis. Again, the Bangladeshi characteristics would increase the risks of working-class outcomes relative to white non-migrants: if they had the same ethnic group effect as Pakistanis their expectations of working-class outcomes on the basis of their characteristics from either class origin would be very different from the Pakistanis' chances.

This distinction is important given the tendency to group the Pakistanis and Bangladeshis together in both published tables and discussion. A focus on changing the characteristics (that is, increasing educational levels) and reducing the links between origins and destination more generally may be effective in breaking the transmission of disadvantage for Bangladeshis, but it looks as if the Pakistanis present specific group-based issues. As mentioned previously, some of these may be to do with geographical issues, the relevance of family structure (although that is a comparable issue for Bangladeshis) and the different meaning of some of the controls for different groups. For example, owner occupation at origin is not necessarily the

indicator of advantage for Pakistanis that it tends to be for other groups (Phillips, 1997).

What can religion add?

Finally, this chapter explores whether religious affiliation makes a difference to social class outcomes, and, if so, how this might add to our understanding of differences within or between groups. Ethnicity per se may not have overwhelming explanatory power, but perhaps, as has been posited by some commentators, religion may be a more telling differentiator between groups, whether because it better captures the specific histories and experiences of particular groups, or because it is a greater source, as some have argued, of group-targeted discrimination (see, for example, Modood, 1997c). First, the relationship between religion and ethnicity was examined simply by identifying the levels of overlap between particular religious affiliations and ethnic groups. As Figure 3.6 shows, over 90% of Pakistanis and Bangladeshis are Muslims, although around a third of Muslims are not from either of these groups.

Figure 3.6: Overlap between religion and ethnic group for certain groups and religions

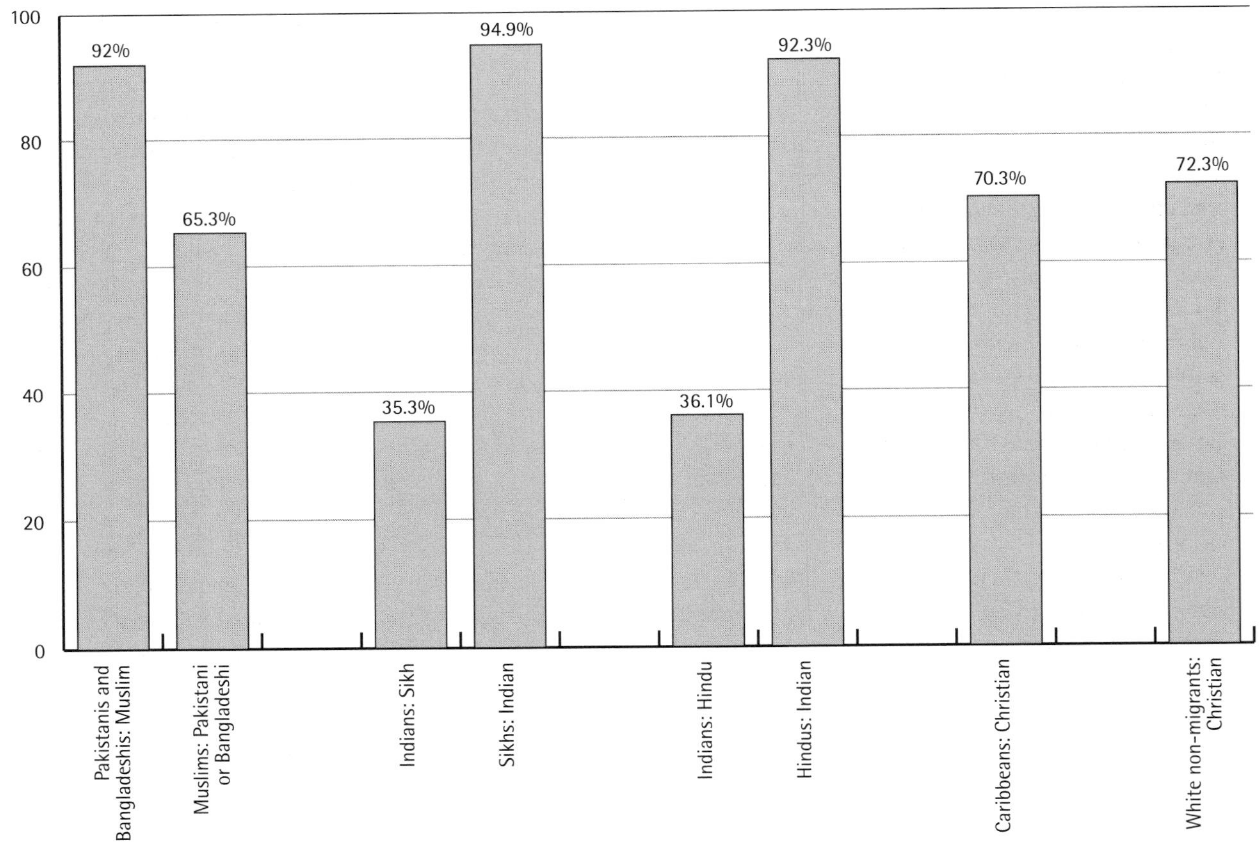

Source: ONS LS, author's analysis

Roughly a third of Indians are Sikh and a third Hindu; the remainder includes Muslims (11%) and Christians (7%). But almost all Hindus and Sikhs claim Indian as their ethnic group. Figure 3.6 also gives the proportions affiliated to a Christian denomination from both the Caribbean and the white non-migrant groups. In both cases just over 70% are affiliated.

Moving on to look at the associations between religion and patterns of origins and destinations, the role of religion in affecting professional/managerial class outcomes compared to any other destination, was analysed controlling for the standard set of factors identified above. The results from this analysis are reported in Table A3 in the Appendix and are described and discussed here.

The inclusion of religion in addition to the control variables (but excluding ethnicity) showed a significant contribution to model fit, and significant effects were found for Hindu, Jewish, Muslim, Sikh and other religions, relative to being a Christian. Being Hindu or Jewish enhanced the probability of a professional/managerial class outcome, other things being equal, while being Muslim, Sikh or from a religious group other than the main religions made such a destination less likely. I examined the effects associated with religion as it varied by sex and found that the disadvantage associated with being Muslim was particularly pronounced for women, possibly lending support to the suggestion made above that some Pakistani (and Bangladeshi) women may have different occupational trajectories, and for some marriage may represent an alternative outcome to occupational success.

The number of significant differentiations between religions indicate that religion is possibly a more stable (and meaningful?) indicator of identity than the ethnic group as normally measured (see, for example, Jacobsen, 1997, 1998). Moreover, the fact that it was not compulsory to complete this one census question may mean that those who did respond have a reasonably distinct sense of their religious identity. The religious differences also indicate diversity within groups: the Indian ethnic group is made up largely of both Sikhs and Hindus, but the two groups' chances of achieving professional/managerial class outcomes are respectively less than and greater than their white counterparts', controlling for relevant factors. This gave us the net result of a non-significant effect for Indians when examining ethnic group effects on their own. Such differentiations indicate the way

that religion can refine our understanding of ethnicity, revealing within-group patterns and processes. The large positive effect for the Jewish group (which would usually be subsumed within the white ethnic group) is particularly striking. Holding a range of relevant characteristics constant, they have much greater chances of class success than their Christian counterparts. Thus we can potentially identify subsets of the classified ethnic groups with distinctive pre-migration histories, within-England and Wales experiences and differential access to resources and different forms of 'capital', including ethnic capital (Borjas, 1992; Modood, 2004), where such subgroups have distinctive religious affiliations.

Moreover, the results could also indicate the extent to which the controls do not cover all the relevant structural and historical differences between groups. Indeed, by contrast with the way ethnic group has been defined in this study, religion on its own does not account for distinctions between migrants and non-migrants, at least in the shorter term, and time since migration might also be important.

To look at the relationship between ethnic group and religion, ethnic group was added back into the model, but *in addition* to religion. With ethnic group included, both the positive effect of being Jewish and the negative effect of being affiliated to the composite group of 'other' religions remained comparable to those when only religion was included. This is not entirely surprising as the Jewish effect and the 'other religious group' effect will be distinguishing primarily within the white non-migrant group (although being Jewish might also be expected to differentiate within the white migrant group). Those belonging to other religions will also be from a mixture of backgrounds, but predominantly white ones. Why other religious background should be associated with lower chances of professional/managerial class attainment, even when controlling for ethnic group differences as well as other relevant characteristics, remains an intriguing question. It may be best considered by exploring what other characteristics are also associated with those affiliating to the range of different religions that make up this residual category (in order of size in England and Wales as a whole, Spiritualists, Pagans, Jain, Wicca, Rastafarian, Bahá'i and Zoroastrian). For example, we can note that this residual category does appear to experience above-average rates of sickness and disability which could impact on their class position (ONS, 2004b).

For the Hindus, the result of including ethnic group alongside religion is to make the effect of being Hindu on the chances of success negative but non-significant. Instead, the Indian ethnic group showed a relatively large and highly significant positive impact on the chances of professional/managerial destinations. Meanwhile, the negative and significant Sikh effect increased in size. What we seem to be seeing then is two groups within the Indian group. First there is a section with greater than anticipated movement into the professional classes – even controlling for education, which is seen as the typical route for Indian upward mobility. Some, although not all, of these will be Hindus, and many may be the East African Asians,[8] who tend to define themselves as Indian and whose particular success has been noted (Modood, 1997a, 1997b).[9] The other section, which has lower than expected probabilities of professional/managerial class destinations, would appear to correspond roughly to the Sikh members of this ethnic group (and possibly the Muslim members also, although this cannot be observed directly here).

Differences within the Indian group are explored further below, but first, turning to the Pakistani and Bangladeshi effects, we find that they are not significant once religion is incorporated into the model (although direction of the Pakistani effect continues to indicate lower chances of a successful outcome). This is hardly surprising, as we saw earlier that over 90% of Pakistanis defined themselves as Muslims, and Muslim religious affiliation is strongly associated with lower chances of professional/managerial outcomes, other things being equal. Thus, for these groups, religion and ethnicity appear to be effectively interchangeable.

To confirm the speculated differences within the Indian group and to investigate whether the disadvantage associated with being Muslim is strictly coterminous with Bangladeshi and Pakistani

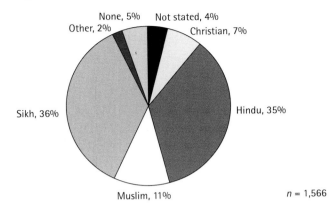

Figure 3.7: Religious breakdown of Indian ethnic group

None, 5% Not stated, 4%
Other, 2% Christian, 7%
Sikh, 36% Hindu, 35%
Muslim, 11% n = 1,566

Source: ONS LS, author's analysis

ethnicity or whether it is a more general effect that impacts on Muslims for other ethnic groups as well, it makes more sense to examine the role of religion for different ethnic groups rather than including both in the same overall analysis. The potential for such analyses was restricted by sample sizes, but some results were nevertheless obtained. Those relating to the Indian group are discussed here. First, Figure 3.7 shows the proportions of different religions within the Indian ethnic group category for the study members. As it shows, the two main religious groups are Hindus and Sikhs, with over a third share each, followed by Muslims making up just over one in 10, and with Christians making up the fourth largest religious group.

Examining the impact of religion within this Indian group and controlling for the standard set of other characteristics showed that both Sikhs and Muslims had significantly lower chances of achieving professional/managerial class outcomes than the other religious groups, although the inclusion of religion itself barely increased the fit of the model. (Full results from this analysis are reported in Table A4 in the Appendix.) Figure 3.8 shows the predicted probabilities of being in the professional/managerial classes for Indians from the five largest religious affiliations (including no religion). The characteristics of those from the different religions vary, so these probabilities reflect not only the independent effect of religion but also the different characteristics (for example, higher/lower educational level, differences in origin class) that accompany the different religious groupings. The figure shows the much lower probabilities of professional/managerial outcomes for Sikhs and even more so for Muslims, and the confidence intervals that accompany the estimates show that there is no overlap in predicted probabilities

---

[8] 21% of Hindus, 9% of Muslims, but only 6% of Sikhs had been born in East Africa according to the 2001 Census (ONS, 2004b). Given the respective sizes of these religious groups and ignoring African Asians from other religions and the British-born children of the East African Asians, this means that roughly half of the East African Asians are Muslim, a little under half are Hindu and under 10% are Sikh.

[9] Although East African Asian success has typically been explained through parental characteristics and motivation to make use of education for upward mobility – both of which are controlled for (even if imperfectly) here.

Figure 3.8: Predicted probabilities of professional/managerial class outcomes for Indians according to their religion

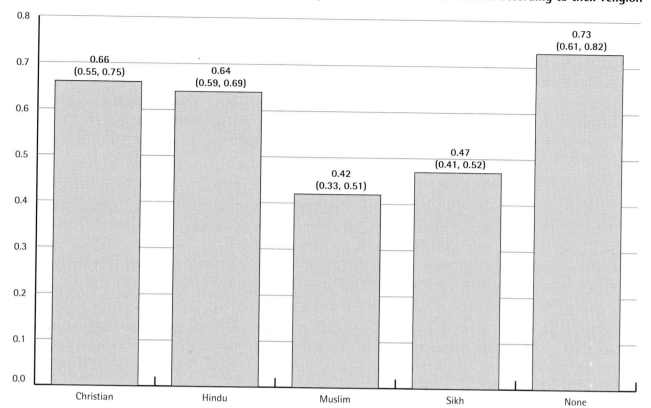

Source: ONS LS, author's analysis

between the three more successful and the two less successful religious groups.

These findings give some support to the hypothesis that it is Muslims who are peculiarly disadvantaged and that we should consider the disadvantage of Pakistanis and Bangladeshis in that light. On the other hand, the Indian Sikhs are shown to be not much better off than the Indian Muslims, which emphasises, instead, the diversity of experiences within supposed ethnic groups, diversity which needs to be related to migration histories and other characteristics of these ethno-religious groupings. Such characteristics are not fully observed or accounted for in this study, but this analysis shows that they serve to differentiate subgroups. Simply to replace ethnic group categories with religious categories does not do justice to this diversity. Combining them, however, enables us to explore within-group variation further, to challenge existing assumptions about groups and to raise further questions for study.

In conclusion, investigations using ethnic group information can be informative on some levels (where the interaction was revealing about the Caribbean experience), while information about religion can create complementary developments in our understanding of the complexity of class processes and group differences within these.

4

Conclusions

This Report began by asking about the relative importance of family origins and ethnic group for shaping children's social class destinations. The Introduction pointed out that, in debates concerning equality of opportunity, the continuing relevance of privileged origins to ensuring better occupational outcomes for children has been seen as at variance with such equality. On the other hand, it is regarded as important to respect parents' right and commitment to do the best for their children, and this is likely to result in the perpetuation of privilege. Moreover, if we look at sub-groups in the population, and particularly those which have experience of marginalisation, such as minority ethnic groups, their ability to draw on individual and group resources, to maintain any class or occupational advantage they achieve, and to transmit such benefits to their children, is indicative of greater openness of society in relation to ethnic difference. Thus a society may reveal high levels of stratification in class terms but, if such patterns are mimicked across different groups, that suggests that racial inequality is less of an issue than class inequality. Conversely, the lack of ability to transmit class privilege across generations within a potentially marginalised group indicates the susceptibility of that group to discrimination and other specifically group-based processes.

The study therefore sought to discover first whether there was evidence that family origins continued to be important for social class destinations across the current generation as a whole and, second, whether the impact of these origins was replicated across minority groups.

In addition, given the substantial evidence discussed relating to the impact of discrimination on migrants' occupational and residential experience on arrival in Britain, apparent upward mobility within minority groups between parents and children can potentially be viewed as compensation for parental downward mobility on migration. Such upward mobility is no less a success story for the groups concerned, but can additionally suggest that downward mobility was experienced by the parents, and that society is becoming more open to the group over time.

This, in turn, leads us to consider the processes by which such upward mobility is achieved. Mobilisation of alternative parental resources, such as networks, parental education, and so on, is one aspect; and the effective use of education, or rather the attainment of educational qualifications, is another. Educational qualifications have been shown to be both a route to success (and upward mobility) for the working classes and also a means by which privileged classes maintain that privilege. Again, within minority groups, the use of education can reveal that particular ethnic group's success; but can also demonstrate the means by which compensation for previous (or on-going) patterns of discrimination are achieved, and can indicate the openness of the education system to be utilised by the group to advance its position. Moreover, the relative weight of educational qualifications across groups in contributing to social class success can be evaluated. Unequal impact of qualifications can be taken to indicate that society is less open to some groups and that 'ethnicity' outweighs more objective measures. On the other hand, while the apparently equalising effect of education can suggest that ethnic inequality is not a major concern once groups are competing in the labour market, the levels of education achieved may still be influenced by ethnic inequalities within the education system. Comparing 'like with like' in terms of the relationship between social class outcomes and education may not be that meaningful if some groups are not very 'like' others in their levels of educational achievement.

It is in light of these general points about what particular relationships and findings mean – or might mean – that we should consider the main results stemming from this Report.

First (in Chapter 2), we saw that the patterns of transition between parents' social class and children's were highly differentiated by ethnic group. In absolute terms some groups ended up in a better position than others – Indians did better than all other groups considered – and rates of transition also varied widely, with patterns of higher class retention, that is the ability of privilege to maintain itself across generations, being stronger for some groups (white non-migrants, Indians and white migrants) and weaker for others (Caribbeans and Pakistanis). This indicates that social class background does play a role in outcomes: class matters. The extent to which ethnic group matters, that is, whether minority group transitions mimic those of the majority, varies, however, with the particular group. Ethnicity appears to be more salient for Caribbeans and Pakistanis than for other groups, indicating that racial inequality is to a certain extent particularised by group and cannot simply be generalised across all those of non-UK-born parentage.

The impact of social class origins and the relative role of ethnic group was further pursued in Chapter 3. Here, other aspects of origins – parents' educational qualifications and economic status of household as well as parents' social class – were held constant, and the analysis revealed that all had independent effects on the chances of ending up in the highest aggregate social class (professional or managerial classes). These effects of origins on social class destinations remained, although reduced in size, when the children's own educational qualifications were taken into account. This indicates both that one of the ways that class advantage is maintained is through more privileged parents ensuring greater educational success for their children, and that, nevertheless, family origins continue to have an impact on children's success, over and above their educational achievement. We can only speculate about the precise processes involved, which are likely to include networks and the acquisition of relevant cultural capital, as well as, possibly, the differentials within apparently comparable qualifications (for example, degrees from old rather than 'new' universities). What is clear, however, is that in England and Wales, for today's generation of 20- to 40-somethings, class origins continue to matter. Does ethnic group matter too?

Reinforcing the picture from Chapter 2, whether ethnic group membership makes a difference appears to depend on the ethnic group.

Caribbeans, Black Africans, Indians, Chinese and others, and white migrants all obtained upward mobility relative to white non-migrants, taking their origins into account. They had higher chances than their white non-migrant counterparts of ending up in the professional or managerial classes, when comparing like with like. This indicates that there may be some compensation going on for the effects of parents' downward mobility following migration, and that society may be relatively open to minority ethnic groups. Moreover, given that a number of origin factors in addition to social class are taken account of, it suggests some absolute level of 'success' for these groups. However, the picture for the Pakistanis is the reverse. They are less likely than their white counterparts to achieve success even when origins are taken account of, they are doing worse than a model of parity of class processes would suggest and thus, for this group, ethnicity far outweighs class in influencing outcomes. This particular ethnic group effect is also increased in magnitude when education is taken account of (and it also applies to the Bangladeshis here, too). Not only do class origins not work for these groups, but neither do educational qualifications (and that is setting aside the question of equal treatment within the school system). Not even higher levels of qualifications can bring them the same occupational rewards as their white counterparts; whereas for other groups the route to their greater levels of upward mobility is through education. Getting qualifications would, then, seem an effective means for achieving parity, for compensating for past discrimination and for building success for some groups; but for Pakistanis and Bangladeshis ethnic group effects outweigh any such achievements. Particular ethnicities matter.

Chapter 3 also considered the full range of possible social class destinations to examine whether ethnic group had an effect on other destinations in addition to chances of being in the professional or managerial classes. It showed that Pakistanis and Bangladeshis in particular, but also Caribbeans, had increased risks of unemployment compared with white non-migrants and comparing those with similar origins and educational levels. So even if Caribbeans overall achieve some upward mobility and do this through education, they are not protected either by origins or by education from increased risks of unemployment. It would seem then that this group may be able to achieve some level of parity within the class structure, but that they are kept in more marginal positions within occupations, making them more susceptible to unemployment. When it comes to unemployment, ethnicity also matters for Caribbeans.

Moreover, the very strong relative risks of unemployment for Bangladeshis and Pakistanis show that these ethnic groups are not only inhibited in succeeding in relation to their backgrounds and education, but they also face much higher risks of being out of work. Again, this study can only speculate about processes, which may include: effects of family composition, structure and size; effects of marriage – and post-marriage employment patterns for women; being located in different parts of the aggregate classes (or education categories) used in the analysis; area effects not effectively controlled for by the area variable; discrimination and the impact of racism; and factors associated with different migration histories, including more recent arrival (than some groups) and thus less time to 'catch up'. But whatever the routes to this greater disadvantage, it is clear that they combine to create a particular ethnic group effect for these groups.

For the other ethnic groups, it would seem that, aside from any particular ethnic group effects in the achievement of particular levels of educational qualifications themselves, they are not clearly differentiated from their white non-migrant counterparts once education and origins are held constant. The same routes that are open to success for the white non-migrants appear to be open to them, as long as they are in a position to benefit from the education system. However, introducing religion into the analysis reveals that these general patterns disguise levels of diversity within groups. Breaking down the Indian group according to the religious affiliations of those who define themselves as 'Indian' reveals very different chances of success. The Indian 'success story' is particularly driven by the Hindus (and the Christians) who have high probabilities of achieving professional or managerial class outcomes, whereas the Sikhs and Muslims fare less well. The ability not only to gain educational qualifications but also to use them to achieve success varies not only across but within groups. While this may lead us to be cautious in what we claim for 'ethnicity' and what we attribute to it, it should nevertheless not divert us from concern at the very clear evidence of the inhibitions to social class success associated with particular ethnic groups, notably Pakistanis and Bangladeshis.

References

Alba, R. and Nee, V. (1997) 'Rethinking assimilation theory for a new era of immigration', *International Migration Review*, vol 31, no 4, pp 826-74.

Aldridge, S. (2001) *Social mobility: A discussion paper*, London: Cabinet Office, Performance and Innovation Unit, April.

Allison, P. (2002) *Missing data*, Thousand Oaks, CA: Sage Publications.

Archer, L. and Francis, B. (forthcoming) 'Changing classes? Exploring the role of social class within the identities and achievement of British Chinese pupils', *Sociology*.

Blackwell, L., Lynch, K., Smith, J. and Goldblatt, P. (2003) *Longitudinal Study 1971-2001: Completeness of census linkage*, London: HMSO.

Blair, T. (2001) 'Speech on the Government's agenda for the future', 8 February, available at www.pm.gov.uk/output/Page1579.asp

Borjas, G. (1992) 'Ethnic capital and intergenerational mobility', *Quarterly Journal of Economics*, vol 107, no 1, pp 123-50.

Bottero, W. and Prandy, K. (2000) 'Social reproduction and mobility in Britain and Ireland in the nineteenth and early twentieth centuries', *Sociology*, vol 34, no 2, pp 265-81.

Bourdieu, P. (1997) 'The forms of capital' in A.H. Halsey, H. Lauder, P. Brown and A. Stuart Wells (eds) *Education: Culture, economy, society*, Oxford: Oxford University Press, pp 46-58.

Breen, R. (1998) 'The persistence of class origin inequalities among school leavers in the Republic of Ireland, 1984-1993', *British Journal of Sociology*, vol 49, no 2, pp 275-98.

Breen, R. and Whelan, C. (1993) 'From ascription to achievement? Origins, education and entry to the labour force in the Republic of Ireland during the twentieth century', *Acta Sociologica*, vol 36, no 1, pp 3-17.

Castles, S. (2000) *Ethnicity and globalization*, London: Sage Publications.

Cheng, Y. and Heath, A. (1993) 'Ethnic origins and class destinations', *Oxford Review of Education*, vol 19, no 2, pp 141-65.

Daniel, W.W. (1968) *Racial discrimination in England*, Harmondsworth: Penguin.

DfES (Department for Education and Skills) (2001) *Youth Cohort Study: The activities and experiences of 21 year olds: England and Wales 2000*, SFR 35/2001, 31 August.

Dorsett, R. (1998) *Ethnic minorities in the inner city*, Bristol: The Policy Press.

Erikson, R. and Goldthorpe, J.H. (1993) *The constant flux: A study of class mobility in industrial societies*, Oxford: Clarendon Press.

Galster, G.C., Metzger, K. and Waite, R. (1999) 'Neighbourhood opportunity structures and immigrants' socioeconomic advancement', *Journal of Housing Research*, vol 10, no 1, pp 95-127.

Glass, D.V. (ed) (1954) *Social mobility in Britain*, London: Routledge and Kegan Paul.

Goldthorpe, J. (1997) 'Problems of "meritocracy"', in A.H. Halsey, H. Lauder, P. Brown and A. Stuart Wells (eds) *Education: Culture, economy, society*, Oxford: Oxford University Press, pp 663-82.

Goldthorpe, J.H. with Llewellyn, C. and Payne, C. (1987) *Social mobility and class structure in modern Britain* (2nd edn), Oxford: Clarendon Press.

Gordon, M. (1964) *Assimilation in American life: The role of race, religion and national origins*, Oxford: Oxford University Press.

Goulbourne, H. (1998) *Race relations in Britain since 1945*, Basingstoke: MacMillan.

Halsey, A.H., Heath, A.F. and Ridge, J.M. (1980) *Origins and destinations: Family, class and education in modern Britain*, Oxford: Clarendon Press.

Heath, A. and McMahon, D. (1997) 'Education and occupational attainments: The impact of ethnic origins', in V. Karn (ed) *Ethnicity in the 1991 Census: Volume four: Employment, education and housing among the ethnic minority populations of Britain*, London: Office for National Statistics, pp 91-113.

Heath, A. and McMahon, D. (2005) 'Social mobility of ethnic minorities', in G.C. Loury, T. Modood and S.M. Teles (eds) *Ethnicity, social mobility and public policy: Comparing the US and UK*, Cambridge: Cambridge University Press, pp 393-413.

Heath, A. and Payne, C. (2000) 'Social mobility' in A.H. Halsey with J. Webb (eds) *Twentieth century British social trends*, Basingstoke: Macmillan, pp 254-78.

Heath, A. and Ridge, J. (1983) 'Social mobility of ethnic minorities', *Journal of Biosocial Science Supplement*, vol 8, pp 169-84.

Hout, M. (1984) 'Occupational mobility of black men: 1962 to 1973', *American Sociological Review*, vol 49, no 3, pp 308-22.

Iganski, P. and Payne, G. (1999) 'Socio-economic re-structuring and employment', *British Journal of Sociology*, vol 50, no 2, pp 195-215.

Jacobson, J. (1997) 'Religion and ethnicity: dual and alternative sources of identity among young British Pakistanis', *Ethnic and Racial Studies*, vol 20, no 2, pp 238-56.

Jacobson, J. (1998) *Islam in transition: Religion and identity among British Pakistani youth*, London: Routledge.

Mason, D. (2000) *Race and ethnicity in modern Britain* (2nd edn), Oxford: Oxford University Press.

Mason, D. (2003) *Explaining ethnic differences: Changing patterns of disadvantage in Britain*, Bristol: The Policy Press.

Marmot, M.G., Adelstein, A.M. and Bulusu, L. (1984) *Immigrant mortality in England and Wales 1970-78: Causes of death by country of birth*, London: HMSO.

Marshall, G., Swift, A. and Roberts, S. (1997) *Against the odds? Social class and social justice in industrial societies*, Oxford: Clarendon Press.

Modood, T. (1997a) 'Employment', in T. Modood, R. Berthoud, J. Lakey, J. Nazroo, P. Smith, S. Virdee and S. Beishon (eds) *Ethnic minorities in Britain: Diversity and disadvantage*, London: Policy Studies Institute, pp 83-149.

Modood, T. (1997b) 'Qualifications and English language', in T. Modood, R. Berthoud, J. Lakey, J. Nazroo, P. Smith, S. Virdee and S. Beishon (eds) *Ethnic minorities in Britain: Diversity and disadvantage*, London: Policy Studies Institute, pp 60-82.

Modood, T. (1997c) 'Culture and identity' in T. Modood, R. Berthoud, J. Lakey, J. Nazroo, P. Smith, S. Virdee and S. Beishon (eds) *Ethnic minorities in Britain: Diversity and disadvantage*, London: Policy Studies Institute, pp 290-338.

Modood, T. (2003) 'Ethnic differentials in educational performance', in D. Mason (ed) *Explaining ethnic differences: Changing patterns of disadvantage in Britain*, Bristol: The Policy Press, pp 53-68.

Modood, T. (2004) 'Capitals, ethnic identity and educational qualifications', *Cultural Trends*, vol 13, no 2, pp 1-19.

Modood, T., Berthoud, R., Lakey, J., Nazroo, J., Smith, P., Virdee, S. and Beishon, S. (eds) (1997) *Ethnic minorities in Britain: Diversity and disadvantage*, London: Policy Studies Institute.

National Statistics (2004) *Focus on ethnicity and identity*, London: Office for National Statistics/HMSO (www.statistics.gov.uk/downloads/theme_compendia/foe2004/Ethnicity.pdf).

Nazroo, J. (1997) 'Health and health services', in T. Modood, R. Berthoud, J. Lakey, J. Nazroo, P. Smith, S. Virdee and S. Beishon (eds), *Ethnic minorities in Britain: Diversity and disadvantage*, London: Policy Studies Institute, pp 224-58.

ONS (Office for National Statistics) (2004a) *The national statistics socio-economic classification user manual*, London: HMSO/ONS.

ONS (2004b) *Focus on religion*, London: HMSO.

Park, R.E. (1950) *Race and culture*, Glencoe, IL: Free Press.

Payne, G. (1992) 'Competing views of contemporary social mobility and social divisions', in R. Burrows and C. Marsh (eds) *Consumption and class*, London: Macmillan.

Payne, G. and Roberts, J. (2002) 'Opening and closing the gates: recent developments in male social mobility in Britain', *Sociological Research Online*, vol 6, no 4, available at www.socresonline.org.uk/6/4/payne.html

Phillips, D. (1997) 'The housing position of ethnic minority group home owners' in V. Karn (ed) *Ethnicity in the 1991 Census: Volume four: Employment education and housing among the ethnic minority populations of Britain*, London: The Stationery Office, pp 170-88.

Platt, L. (2002) *Parallel lives? Poverty among ethnic minority groups in Britain*, London: Child Poverty Action Group.

Platt, L. (2005) 'The intergenerational social mobility of minority ethnic groups', *Sociology*, vol 39, no 3, pp 445-61.

Prandy, K. (1998) 'Class and continuity in social reproduction', *Sociological Review*, vol 46, no 2, pp 340-64.

Putnam, R.D. (2000) *Bowling alone: The collapse and revival of American community*, New York, NY: Simon & Schuster.

Robinson, V. (1990) 'Roots to mobility: the social mobility of Britain's black population, 1971-87', *Ethnic and Racial Studies*, vol 13, no 2, pp 274-86.

Savage, M. (2000) *Class analysis and social transformation*, Buckingham: Open University Press.

Smith, D.J. (1977) *Racial disadvantage in Britain: The PEP Report*, Harmondsworth: Penguin.

Solomos, J. (1989) *Race and racism in contemporary Britain*, Basingstoke: Macmillan.

Appendix

Table A1: Logistic regressions of probability of professional/managerial destination in 2001, controlling for individual and background characteristics

	Model 1 Coefficients (SE)	Model 2 Coefficients (SE)	Model 3 Coefficients (SE)	Model 4 Coefficients (SE)	Model 5 Coefficients (SE)
Cohort (baseline is 1971 cohort)	*–0.006 (0.011)*	–0.081 (0.012)	–0.077 (0.012)	–0.236 (0.013)	–0.158 (0.014)
Age (base is 12-15)					
Age group 1	0.053 (0.013)	*0.011 (0.013)*	*0.013 (0.013)*	–0.192 (0.014)	–1.55 (0.015)
Age group 2	0.059 (0.014)	0.041 (0.014)	0.041 (0.014)	–0.049 (0.015)	*–0.024 (0.016)*
Male	*0.022 (0.012)*	*0.015 (0.013)*	*0.015 (0.012)*	0.076 (0.014)	0.047 (0.014)
Partnered	0.986 (0.014)	1.017 (0.014)	1.026 (0.014)	1.135 (0.016)	0.885 (0.017)
Area concentration of minorities (baseline 0%)					
Up to 1%	0.213 (0.020)	0.197 (0.021)	0.192 (0.021)	0.191 (0.023)	0.198 (0.023)
1 to 5%	0.330 (0.023)	0.326 (0.024)	0.301 (0.024)	0.349 (0.026)	0.359 (0.026)
5 to 10%	0.210 (0.033)	0.241 (0.034)	0.189 (0.034)	0.268 (0.037)	0.300 (0.038)
More than 10%	0.221 (0.032)	0.240 (0.032)	0.154 (0.035)	0.266 (0.038)	0.303 (0.039)
Origin class: base is working					
Service-class	1.108 (0.015)	0.534 (0.017)	0.539 (0.017)	0.322 (0.019)	0.296 (0.019)
Intermediate	0.248 (0.016)	0.060 (0.017)	0.061 (0.017)	*0.019 (0.018)*	*–0.012 (0.018)*
Other	–0.266 (0.028)	–0.205 (0.033)	–0.203 (0.033)	–0.096 (0.036)	*–0.038 (0.038)*
Mother's qualifications (base no qualifications)					
No co-resident mother		–0.216 (0.045)	–0.208 (0.045)	–0.123 (0.050)	*–0.065 (0.051)*
Mother with qualifications		0.432 (0.025)	0.420 (0.025)	0.115 (0.027)	0.138 (0.027)
Father's qualifications (base no qualifications)					
No co-resident father		0.224 (0.028)	0.226 (0.028)	0.135 (0.031)	0.132 (0.031)
Father with qualifications		0.535 (0.022)	0.529 (0.022)	0.215 (0.023)	0.221 (0.024)
Tenure at origin (base is owner occupation)					
Local authority		–0.575 (0.015)	–0.570 (0.015)	–0.278 (0.016)	–0.161 (0.017)
Private rented		–0.306 (0.021)	–0.303 (0.021)	–0.159 (0.023)	–0.095 (0.023)
Car ownership at origin (baseline is no cars)					
1 car		0.265 (0.015)	0.274 (0.015)	0.173 (0.017)	0.067 (0.017)
2 or more cars		0.399 (0.021)	0.408 (0.022)	0.290 (0.023)	0.137 (0.024)
Ethnic group (baseline is white non-migrant)					
Caribbean			0.197 (0.068)	*–0.088 (0.073)*	*0.060 (0.078)*
Black African			0.557 (0.219)	*0.050 (0.232)*	*0.188 (0.236)*
Indian			0.445 (0.062)	*0.078 (0.062)*	*–0.060 (0.063)*
Pakistani			–0.589 (0.093)	–0.885 (0.098)	–0.945 (0.099)
Bangladeshi			*–0.277 (0.223)*	–0.536 (0.219)	*–0.387 (0.229)*
Chinese and other			0.499 (0.100)	*0.095 (0.103)*	*0.118 (0.108)*
White migrant			0.257 (0.041)	*0.070 (0.044)*	*0.050 (0.045)*
Sample member's qualifications (base is 0)					
Lower				1.02 (0.026)	0.849 (0.027)
Middle				1.48 (0.027)	1.29 (0.027)
Further				2.78 (0.028)	2.58 (0.28)
Car ownership at destination (base is 0)					
1 car					0.497 (0.028)
2 or more cars					0.852 (0.029)
Tenure at destination (base is owner occupation)					
Local authority					–1.19 (0.035)
Private rented					–0.479 (0.023)
Constant	–1.37 (0.025)	–1.26 (0.029)	–1.28 (0.030)	–2.63 (0.038)	–2.78 (0.045)
N			134992		
Chi2 Change (df)		1252 (6)	205 (8)	14004(4)	3366 (5)

Notes: Statistically significant results at at least the 0.05 level are highlighted in **bold**; results that are not significant are in *italics*.
Standard errors are adjusted for repeat observations on persons.
The regression models were run both using dummies to represent missing cases and excluding all cases with missing values. The advantage of the former approach is that it maintains the sample size; however, it may do so at the expense of distorting the estimates (Allison, 2002). Therefore, while the results from the models employing dummies are cited here, the models substituting missing values for these dummies have been included in the Technical Appendix (available at www.jrf.org.uk/bookshop). For brevity the coefficients for the dummies are not given in this Table.
Source: ONS LS, author's analysis

Table A2: Multinomial logistic regression of destinations at 2001 controlling for individual and background variables

	Coefficient for intermediate class (SE)	Coefficient for manual/routine (SE)	Coefficient for unemployment class (SE)	Coefficient for 'other' (SE)
Cohort (baseline is 1971 cohort)	0.063 (0.016)	0.374 (0.016)	0.495 (0.038)	0.319 (0.026)
Age (baseline is 12-15)				
Age group 1	0.097 (0.018)	0.279 (0.018)	0.308 (0.040)	0.194 (0.028)
Age group 2	*0.001 (0.019)*	0.089 (0.019)	*0.078 (0.044)*	0.078 (0.030)
Male	−0.089 (0.017)	0.062 (0.017)	0.232 (0.038)	−0.770 (0.028)
Partnered	−0.591 (0.020)	−1.13 (0.019)	−2.322 (0.042)	−2.59 (0.036)
Area concentration of minorities (baseline is 0%)				
Up to 1%	−0.170 (0.027)	−0.203 (0.027)	*−0.128 (0.067)*	−0.236 (0.044)
1 to 5%	−0.255 (0.032)	−0.436 (0.032)	−0.304 (0.077)	−0.391 (0.051)
5 to 10%	−0.164 (0.045)	−0.426 (0.046)	*−0.044 (0.097)*	−0.204 (0.069)
More than 10%	−0.162 (0.046)	−0.424 (0.046)	*−0.076 (0.096)*	−0.165 (0.068)
Class of origin (baseline is working class)				
Service-class	−0.178 (0.023)	−0.478 (0.024)	−0.350 (0.057)	−0.353 (0.040)
Intermediate	0.129 (0.021)	−0.149 (0.022)	−0.141 (0.053)	−0.100 (0.036)
Other	*−0.064 (0.047)*	*−0.066 (0.043)*	0.400 (0.080)	0.476 (0.058)
Mother's qualifications (base no qualifications)				
No co-resident mother	*0.113 (0.062)*	*0.061 (0.060)*	0.342 (0.107)	0.271 (0.083)
Mother with qualifications	−0.132 (0.033)	−0.170 (0.038)	−0.250 (0.086)	0.124 (0.057)
Father's qualifications (base no qualifications)				
No co-resident father	*−0.016 (0.038)*	−0.228 (0.037)	*−0.141 (0.076)*	−0.220 (0.054)
Father with qualifications	−0.202 (0.029)	−0.339 (0.033)	*0.011 (0.074)*	*−0.031 (0.052)*
Tenure at origin (baseline is owner occupation)				
Local authority	0.098 (0.020)	0.377 (0.020)	0.492 (0.044)	0.482 (0.031)
Private rented	0.111 (0.028)	0.205 (0.028)	−0.210 (0.065)	−0.186 (0.046)
Car ownership at origin (base is 0)				
1 car	*−0.011 (0.021)*	−0.245 (0.020)	−0.481 (0.043)	−0.362 (0.030)
2 or more cars	*−0.013 (0.028)*	−0.492 (0.030)	−0.663 (0.069)	−0.554 (0.047)
Ethnic group (baseline is white non-migrant)				
Caribbean	0.185 (0.088)	*−0.163 (0.094)*	0.556 (0.137)	*−0.089 (0.117)*
Black African	*0.090 (0.276)*	*−0.133 (0.299)*	*0.0457 (0.477)*	−0.818 (0.401)
Indian	*0.009 (0.078)*	*−0.122 (0.082)*	*0.062 (0.161)*	*−0.177 (0.128)*
Pakistani	0.777 (0.116)	0.598 (0.127)	1.674 (0.178)	1.545 (0.145)
Bangladeshi	*0.361 (0.285)*	*0.412 (0.256)*	1.491 (0.376)	0.712 (0.364)
Chinese and other	*0.024 (0.129)*	−0.367 (0.148)	*0.295 (0.211)*	*−0.045 (0.193)*
White migrant	*0.029 (0.053)*	−0.195 (0.057)	*0.052 (0.109)*	*0.063 (0.081)*
Sample member's qualifications (base is 0)				
Lower	−0.425 (0.033)	−1.121 (0.029)	−1.573 (0.055)	−1.993 (0.040)
Middle	−0.761 (0.033)	−1.695 (0.030)	−1.992 (0.059)	−2.506 (0.043)
Further	−1.94 (0.035)	−3.243 (0.034)	−3.000 (0.063)	−3.588 (0.047)
Constant	0.671 (0.047)	1.94 (0.045)	0.256 (0.092)	2.198 (0.063)
N		134992		
Wald chi2 (df)		31499 (144)		

Notes: Statistically significant results at at least the 0.05 level are highlighted in **bold**; results that are not significant are in *italics*.
Standard errors are adjusted for repeat observations on persons.
Interpretation: The four columns of results show, for each category of class, the probability, relative to the baseline category for each variable and controlling for the other variables, of being in that class category rather than the professional/managerial class. For example, the coefficient for cohort in the first column shows that those in the 1981 cohort are slightly more likely than those in the 1971 cohort to fall into intermediate class destinations rather than professional/managerial ones. This does not mean that in absolute terms more of the cohort ends up in the intermediate class than in the professional/ managerial class. Rather it means simply that slightly more of them are likely to end up there than is the case for the older cohort, once relevant characteristics are controlled.
Source: ONS LS, author's analysis

Table A3: The effects of religion on professional/managerial destination 2001, controlling for relevant characteristics

	Model 1 Coefficients (SE)	Model 2 Coefficients (SE)	Model 3 Coefficients (SE)
Cohort (baseline is 1971 cohort)	−0.235 (0.013)	−0.234 (0.013)	−0.234 (0.013)
Age (baseline is 12-15)			
Age group 1	−0.193 (0.014)	−0.192 (0.014)	−0.192 (0.014)
Age group 2	−0.049 (0.015)	−0.049 (0.015)	−0.049 (0.015)
Male	0.077 (0.014)	0.077 (0.014)	0.068 (0.016)
Partnered	1.134 (0.016)	1.135 (0.016)	1.134 (0.016)
Area concentration of minorities (baseline is 0%)			
Up to 1%	0.192 (0.023)	0.190 (0.022)	0.192 (0.022)
1 to 5%	0.355 (0.026)	0.347 (0.026)	0.355 (0.026)
5 to 10%	0.279 (0.037)	0.267 (0.037)	0.279 (0.037)
More than 10%	0.290 (0.036)	0.270 (0.038)	0.289 (0.036)
Class of origin (baseline is working class)			
Service-class	0.318 (0.019)	0.319 (0.018)	0.318 (0.019)
Intermediate	*0.019 (0.018)*	*0.018 (0.018)*	*0.019 (0.018)*
Other	−0.095 (0.036)	−0.097 (0.036)	−0.095 (0.036)
Mother's qualifications (base no qualifications)			
No co-resident mother	−0.126 (0.050)	−0.122 (0.050)	−0.126 (0.050)
Mother with qualifications	0.118 (0.027)	0.115 (0.027)	0.119 (0.027)
Father's qualifications (base no qualifications)			
No co-resident father	0.130 (0.015)	0.134 (0.031)	0.131 (0.031)
Father with qualifications	0.217 (0.023)	0.215 (0.023)	0.217 (0.023)
Tenure at origin (baseline is owner occupation)			
Local authority	−0.280 (0.016)	−0.279 (0.016)	−0.279 (0.016)
Private rented	−0.159 (0.023)	−0.159 (0.023)	−0.158 (0.022)
Car ownership at origin (base is 0)			
1 car	0.170 (0.017)	0.173 (0.017)	0.171 (0.017)
2 or more cars	0.285 (0.023)	0.288 (0.023)	0.285 (0.023)
Sample member's qualifications (base is 0)			
Lower	1.019 (0.026)	1.018 (0.026)	1.018 (0.026)
Middle	1.478 (0.027)	1.476 (0.027)	1.477 (0.027)
Further	2.777 (0.028)	2.774 (0.028)	2.777 (0.028)
Religion (base = Christian)			
Not stated	*−0.050 (0.031)*	*−0.052 (0.031)*	*−0.024 (0.044)*
Buddhist	*−0.122 (0.170)*	*−0.145 (0.171)*	*0.236 (0.249)*
Hindu	0.190 (0.097)	*−0.211 (0.140)*	0.273 (0.132)
Jewish	0.377 (0.122)	0.372 (0.122)	0.541 (0.172)
Muslim	−0.736 (0.075)	−0.668 (0.127)	−0.922 (0.111)
Sikh	−0.204 (0.098)	−0.611 (0.146)	*−0.194 (0.138)*
Other	−0.299 (0.118)	−0.324 (0.119)	−0.339 (0.168)
None	*−0.007 (0.018)*	*−0.006 (0.018)*	*−0.041 (0.026)*
Ethnic group (base is white non-migrant)			
Caribbean		*−0.077 (0.073)*	
Black African		*0.100 (0.233)*	
Indian		0.447 (0.115)	
Pakistani		*−0.275 (0.154)*	
Bangladeshi		*0.088 (0.252)*	
Chinese and other		*0.170 (0.105)*	
White migrant		*0.081 (0.044)*	
Religion interacted with sex			
Not stated by male			*−0.046 (0.061)*
Buddhist by male			*−0.599 (0.340)*
Hindu by male			*−0.172 (0.189)*
Jewish by male			*−0.331 (0.244)*
Muslim by male			0.356 (0.244)
Sikh by male			*−0.017 (0.192)*
Other by male			*0.085 (0.236)*
None by male			0.061 (0.035)
Constant	−2.620 (0.038)	−2.624 (0.038)	−2.616 (0.038)
N	134978		
Wald test for inclusion of religion/ethnic group variables: chi square (df)	122 (8)	39 (8)	

Notes: Statistically significant results at least the 0.05 level are highlighted in **bold**; results that are not significant are in *italics*.
Standard errors are adjusted for repeat observations on persons.
Source: ONS LS, author's analysis

Table A4: The effects of religion on professional/managerial destination 2001 among Indians, controlling for relevant characteristics

	Coefficient (SE)
Cohort (baseline is 1971 cohort)	–0.258 (0.150)
Age (baseline is 12-15)	
Age group 1	**–0.312 (0.149)**
Age group 2	–0.164 (0.150)
Male	–0.082 (0.129)
Partnered	**0.979 (0.154)**
Area concentration of minorities greater than 1% (*baseline is 0-1%*)	–0.289 (0.333)
Class of origin (baseline is working class)	
Service-class	0.236 (0.237)
Intermediate	–0.117 (0.215)
Other	–0.069 (0.294)
Mother's qualifications (base no qualifications)	
No co-resident mother	–0.048 (0.406)
Mother with qualifications	0.494 (0.379)
Father's qualifications (base no qualifications)	
No co-resident father	0.318 (0.365)
Father with qualifications	0.021 (0.252)
Tenure at origin (baseline is owner occupation)	
Local authority	**0.892 (0.254)**
Private rented	0.275 (0.246)
Car ownership at origin (base is 0)	
1 car	0.220 (0.141)
2 or more cars	0.137 (0.247)
Sample member's qualifications (base is none)	
Lower	**1.776 (0.332)**
Middle	**2.295 (0.333)**
Further	**3.962 (0.337)**
Religion (base =Christian)	
Not stated	–0.367 (0.404)
Hindu	–0.161 (0.265)
Muslim	**–0.635 (0.309)**
Sikh	**–0.531 (0.270)**
Other	0.559 (0.583)
None	–0.423 (0.370)
Constant	**–2.421 (0.534)**
N	1546
Wald test for inclusion of religion: chi square (df)	12.6 (6)

Notes: Statistically significant results at at least the 0.05 level are highlighted in **bold**; results that are not significant are in *italics*.
Standard errors are adjusted for repeat observations on persons.
Source: ONS LS, author's analysis

For enquiries or renewal at
Quarles LRC
Tel: 01708 455011 – Extension 4009